Born a Poor Black, Indian, White Girl

Overcoming Childhood Trauma and Living a Spiritual Life

De Fletcher

Spirit Oaks
PRESS

Published by Spirit Oaks Press

Paperback Edition
ISBN: 978-1-7379507-4-5

Cover Design By: Matt Davies

To my brother Charlie . . .
Thank you for blessing me with your presence for
thirty-seven years.
See you when I get to the Other Side.

Contents

Contents (2)

Preface

The original *Born a Poor, Black, Indian, White Girl* was first published four years ago (in Ebook and paperback). Its mission is to assist adults who have experienced childhood trauma. Its goal is to help those same adults realize they are not alone with their grief, drama, stress, or trauma. The true-life stories (and lessons learned) are about healing old wounds survivors carry with them into adulthood.

Shortly after I published this book with its original title, I changed the title because I felt pressure from others telling me it wasn't politically correct. I cried the day I changed the title to *Simply Unbreakable*. The new title was good, but it wasn't THE title.

For the next two years, every time I thought about (or talked to someone about my book), it made me sad. I don't know how to explain it other than it seemed wrong. I no longer recognized the book I had poured so much time and energy into. So, in 2020, I made things right by restoring the original title.

This original title represents my struggle with the <u>identity confusion</u> and trauma that plagued me throughout my childhood and into adulthood. It is the title I gave it years before the book was even written. The title that chose me many years ago. I knew instantly it was the only one suitable for my story.

The last four years, I've remembered more stories and tidbits from this part of my life. I wanted to include them in this revised paperback edition. Some of the stories will make you laugh and others may bring tears. Most will take you to a place where you can look inside yourself and find answers.

This *2022 Paperback Edition* includes more stories, lessons learned, and insights into how I overcame childhood trauma.

May these stories resonate with you and may you find some healing for your life in the words shared within.

Introduction

If you haven't experienced more than brief moments of happiness because of past abuse or trauma, you're not alone! You may do everything you know how, but your life isn't what you thought it would be. Perhaps you don't even realize your unhappiness stems from unreleased stress, drama, grief, or trauma. Maybe you believe there is too much drama to overcome and have a happy life.

If this sounds like you or your life, I get it. I've been down that road more than once. I struggled for years to overcome my childhood trauma that cast a shadow over my adult life. Not everything adults taught me, I believed and experienced, helped me as an adult. Hopefully, reading about my journey will give you a key that frees you from any past you may carry around.

This story is about discovering my true self among the cultures, prejudices, and abuse I experienced growing up. It's also about me as a woman and how I overcame the shadows of my past. I'm sharing where I've been, what I've learned (and relearned several times), and my observations along the way. It's a funny, sarcastic, contemplative, sad struggle between living the way I was taught and what I felt in my soul was right.

The funny stuff I couldn't make up if I tried. It may have you laughing so hard that your stomach hurts. Perhaps it will remind you of a hilarious story that happened to you.

The heartbreaking experiences may bring up some grief for you as well. Maybe you'll be able to do some healing while reading these words. Regardless of our differences, we all have experiences in common because we've all gone through them at some point.

It took a major wake-up call to lead me to discover my true nature, what makes me happy, and what I wanted to do with my life. This event also prompted me to let go of beliefs and automatic responses that were keeping me unhappy and creating drama and lack in my life.

I've done my best to recall exactly every story and detail in this book. Some events are as clear as the day they happened. Others are a little "fuzzy" in my mind. For whatever reason, blocks of time are missing from my memory banks. I suspect this is because of traumas that are best left unremembered. I also may capture a glimpse in time, a thought, or a snapshot.

The way I share these words with you may seem unconventional. I write the way I talk, so reading this book will be like listening to your best friend share stories about their life. I also use southern terms (or slang), so some words or phrases may not be familiar to you. Read them from a regional, historical perspective. I've also used words from various Native American cultures which are capitalized because of their cultural significance.

I'm choosing to talk about where I'm from and what I've lived through. I may be serious one moment and humorous the next.

So, if you read something you don't like, just remember . . . I've been there, done that, got the t-shirt, and it's just my perspective.

Throughout this book, I will also share some specifics about the places I grew up (like areas, street names, etc.). After all, this is also a true, southern, hometown story about overcoming childhood adversity. Readers who live here will relate to the setting.

This book is about how I overcame a myriad of childhood traumas that brought me to where I am today. I share it knowing that some parts will resonate with every person who reads it. Perhaps it will help you overcome something in your life that is holding you back or keeping you down. I hope everyone will read the words with an open mind and approach them, intending to learn something. If you do, I'm positive you'll find at least one thing that speaks to you or one thing you've needed to hear.

This is the story of my life's journey. I'm sharing my struggles, pain, grief, and humor with you so you can see you're not alone. Once we realize we're not alone, we can begin releasing the past and finding the better, happier life we deserve. I share what I've learned, experienced, dreamed, and made come true. May you enjoy it fully and may it resonate with where you've been, where you are, and where you want to be.

People of the Rainbow . . .
Your skin has many colors, but I see your heart is
Red.

The work you do in silence will bring us back to
peace.

And so shall we walk in beauty all the days of our
lives.

1
The Pox
and the Pedophile

I have often wondered what the weather was like on my birth day. Was it hot and sunny with a blue sky and big, white, puffy clouds? Were there thunderstorms with lots of lightning, rain, and wind? I lean toward it being stormy since I've always had a kinship with the power of a summer thunderstorm. Either way, my impatience to be born (and my mom's lack of timing) threw my entire birth process off. I popped out in the backseat of a taxi on the way to the hospital! Apparently, I could not wait to experience the humid, semi-deep south of Arkansas!

My birth certificate reads, "En route to St. Vincent's Infirmary" as my place of birth. I guess the Department of Health wasn't about to put "Yellow Cab #62" on the official birth record. Did being born in a taxi create the lifetime traveler I've become? I'm not sure, but I've often pondered that question. I suspect it planted a small seed of exploration deep within my psyche.

That is how I entered this world. A somewhat impatient, blue-eyed baby girl. One destined (it would seem) to travel before I breathed my first breath. I was a brand new human with my whole life ahead of me. A perfectly created human with an inherent sense of love, exploration, laughter, and imagination . . . just like all babies.

For whatever reason, I remember little about my earliest years. Blocks of time were plucked from my memory. Perhaps there were too many events to remove them one-by-one. Maybe I suffered some illness or trauma that affected my memory. Who can say for sure? My mother or other family members revealed no such illness or trauma to me. In between these vast blank spaces of my early childhood, three moments in time stand out in my mind:

1. Chickenpox.
2. Sexual abuse.
3. Getting a special birthday gift from my grandma.

From a kindergartener's perspective, having chickenpox felt like the worst thing ever! It was difficult to deal with the oozing sores and constant itching. There was nothing anyone could do except wait until the disease ran its course.

I also learned how sympathetic, concerned, and crabby grown-ups can be when caring for sick children. Dealing with my miserable "ickiness" daily wore on my mom and the older lady taking care of me.

They couldn't wait for things to return to normal. I don't know how long my pox lasted. I do remember wishing (every day) it would go away.

"He gained my trust and then took advantage."

After what seemed like forever, the red, oozy sores went away. I felt so much better! I'd managed not to infect my siblings, so I was allowed back into the tribe. The adults breathed a sigh of relief and, like "presto!", the daily mega-dose of crabbiness went away. Being healthy again felt great. Life went on, but it wasn't long before I realized chickenpox wasn't the worst thing ever.

It's difficult to talk about childhood sexual trauma, but I believe it's important to get it out into the open. The benefit of doing so far outweighs any discomfort on my part. My memory of this event didn't surface until after I had written the original manuscript of this book. Initially, I decided not to include it in my story. It seemed insignificant, but I have since realized its importance as the genesis of a recurring pattern during my childhood.

It seems I was around six years old when my mom's fiancé sat me on his lap. As a child, I thought it was a sign of affection. I don't remember anyone else being around when it happened. At first, he was just talking to me and asking me things. After a few minutes, I could feel his fingers touching my private area.

I didn't know what was happening. One of his fingers went inside me and I felt pressure there for a bit. At some point, I experienced a tingling feeling where his fingers were playing with me. It sort of felt like I needed to go to the bathroom really badly. All the while, he continued talking to me like nothing else was going on.

My memory has only revealed one event with this person. I don't recall what happened after this one event. Did he keep having his little "talks" with me? This man was in our lives for a year (it seems). My best guess would be if it happened once, it happened multiple times. Perhaps the complete story isn't accessible to me at this time. I consider that a good thing.

It's funny the things we remember and how we remember them. For me, enormous blocks of time are missing from childhood. Maybe it's part of my defense mechanism that locked away those blocks for my protection. Maybe I don't need to remember everything, but I remember the name of my first abuser. His name was Tom Deo. My mom referred to him as her "big Indian". It seems like she said he was an actual Native American from Oklahoma. The probability of him being alive today is slim, but it is cathartic just saying the name aloud.

I've wondered many times how an adult can sexually assault little girls (or boys). What made it worse for me was that it was under the guise of playing, hugging, tickling, etc. He gained my trust and then took advantage.

Many times I've wondered if he did the same to my other sisters. I've read that most pedophiles have an age preference. It seems his preference was around six years old (give or take). A six-year-old doesn't understand what this type of abuse is. They wouldn't have the awareness to realize it was wrong and tell someone.

"Memories are potent things. They have power."

My mom and Tom never got married. Perhaps they weren't a good match. Maybe she caught him doing something to one of her daughters. I don't know for sure. (I just remembered mom telling us she found out he was already married and broke off the engagement.) Now I have questions popping up in my mind. Did he have children? If so, were his children not his "type" so he went looking elsewhere? Had he molested his own children until they got too old for him?

Now, I'm not a licensed mental health practitioner or law enforcement expert, but I would like to share what I've learned from this part of my life experience. I share it with you so you will know how to avoid creating a situation that endangers the health and wellbeing of your children.

My best piece of advice for single parents is watch that new person in your life who says they'll help raise/watch your kids. Why are they okay with it?

Do they have children of their own? Have they spent a lot of time with your children and grown to love them? Watch them! Do they often volunteer (you don't have to ask them) to do tasks where they will be alone with your children? This includes bathing, dressing, tucking in bed, babysitting, changing diapers, day trips, etc. Watch them carefully! Sometimes their helpfulness comes in the guise of giving you a break or more time to yourself. You won't know what his or her type is, but you can bet it's right around the age of your child!

Pedophiles know it takes time to gain trust, so their type may be six months (or so) from the age of your child. I don't believe there are any age limits for pedophiles. Any child of any age or background is fair game for these predators! They know where they can find the children they prefer. They work (or hunt) in those places! You can bet they will be close to any place with children. If they can become part of a family (where secrets can be kept), it's the safest way for them to abuse. Pedophiles (or other abusers) can be men or women, so protect your children! I'm not saying every person who comes into a single parent's life is a pedophile or abuser. What I am saying is parents must be very careful with whom they allow access to their children! Adults must understand that pedophiles exist at every level of society. There are no safe places!

As a child I often heard, "You have to take the good with the bad." Maybe it's just a southern life lesson statement parents repeat to their children.

Perhaps it instills an understanding that life isn't all roses and good times. Could it be they passed it down for generations and at some point no one knew what it meant, but they kept repeating it, anyway? I'm not sure I understand what all it's supposed to mean. In my case, the pox and the pedophile qualify for the bad, and my grandma giving me a special birthday gift was the good.

Grandma gifted me a pair of saddle shoes when I was six years old. They were the best shoes ever! (Cheerleaders wore shoes like that with their team color on each side. The saddle shoes just came in black or brown.) Man, I felt like I was something else wearing those shoes around! I had wanted a pair for what seemed like an eternity. I was proud of those shoes! Maybe I liked those shoes so much because my grandma gave them to me. She was my favorite person in the whole, wide world!

I don't recall what happened to those shoes, but I bet I wore them until I couldn't stuff my feet into them any longer! It seems the best gifts are given out of genuine love and the giver expects nothing in return. When it's all said and done, it's not about the gift. It's about the positive feelings and good times shared with those you love.

The gift of those shoes taught me how important it is to spend time with your loved ones. Memories are potent things. They have power. They can keep a family close through tough times. This power also keeps our loved ones in our hearts when they leave this world, but that's a story for later on.

Although I don't recall how I got the scar on my left forearm, I do remember getting my foot stuck under the chain-link fence on the school playground. I earned a scar for that one and a scar on my left knee from a car accident.

Once, my brother pulled me around the yard by my arm until it came out of the socket. That was the first time I remember experiencing intense physical pain. These are the kind of tidbits I remember from my early years. Just random bits tucked in between blank spaces. As time went on, it became abundantly clear I was other things. Things so far removed from that once perfect baby, I couldn't fathom their depths.

What Early Childhood Taught Me

1. Any abuse you experienced as a child is NOT your fault! You did nothing to deserve it! There was nothing you could have done to stop it!
2. You can choose any day to tell your story and bring your abusers to justice.
3. You can choose any moment to release the pain. To forgive yourself for thinking it had anything to do with you.
4. The happy life you've always wanted awaits you on the other side of letting go of the past.
5. You're not alone! Many people (just like you) have experienced childhood trauma. Find support to help you during your letting go time!

6. Spend time with the ones you love and make wonderful memories you can save for later.

7. Your childhood experiences do not have to negatively affect the rest of your life. Make sure they don't.

What Pedophiles Taught Me

1. Parents must be very careful with whom they allow access to their children! (Potential partners, friends, neighbors, teachers, and more.)

2. Do a background check on anyone who may be alone with your child BEFORE they are allowed to be alone with them!

3. Watch closely how a person interacts with your children BEFORE you allow them to be alone with them!

4. Adults MUST pay attention so they'll know when something is off about a person.

5. Parents MUST understand that most pedophiles wear a mask. They pretend to be good people, nice, agreeable, helpful with the kids, etc. It is a show they put on to get to your children!

6. Single parents (and especially single moms) are a target. NEVER allow someone you have not checked out thoroughly to be alone with your children, EVER! It DOES NOT matter how much you'd like alone time, a night on the town, or a mini vacation!

7. Unless your abusers are dead or behind bars, they are still abusing children.

8. All adults are responsible for protecting our children (whether they are your children or not)!

9. Never, ever witness a child being abused or being taken and not say or do something!

All this time . . .
All those years . . .
All the pain . . .
All the tears . . .
All for what is to come.

2
Racism and Black Moments

When I was young, I played outside with the other neighborhood kids. We would play games like chase, hopscotch, kickball, hand-jive rhymes, or double-dutch. We simply did what kids inherently want to do (explore, discover, socialize, and have fun). It seemed like everyone knew everybody else. We rode our bikes around, played hide-and-seek, and never worried about a thing. All the parents watched out for the kids. We all knew we'd better be home before dark or else we'd catch heck.

Life seemed cool and funny back then. Sometimes we would laugh so hard we couldn't stop and fall to the ground, holding our stomachs. Other times we would hang out on auntie's or mama's porch and just talk about funny stuff that had happened or things our parents had said or done. Believe me, kids know so much more than adults think they do. They are like sponges and soak up everything going on around them.

Kids are like walking, talking video recorders, so parents should be careful with what they say around them.

After I started school, playtime shifted to the weekends and holiday/summer breaks. We would get home around 3:30 p.m. and finish any homework before supper. After supper, we'd take a bath, get our clothes ready for the next day, and go to bed early. (It's easier to learn if a child is well-rested.) It took a while getting used to this new routine. Life wasn't as much fun as it was before.

My first day of school felt like I was on a new adventure! I got to walk to school with my sister and brother. I also got my first good look at my elementary school. It was huge, with a massive staircase leading up to the front entrance. It was an architectural masterpiece when it was built and named after our nation's 100th birthday. All the cool colors, pictures, numbers, and letters our teacher used during my first weeks of first grade amazed me. It was all so fascinating, and was I eager to learn! There were lots of kids that went to our centennial school. Some were a lot bigger than me. I think they were fifth and sixth graders. They almost seemed like grownups!

Life changed shortly after I started first grade. I didn't realize what was happening at first, but having fun changed. We still had fun (if everything was calm in the neighborhood), but we didn't hang out with all the kids like we used to when we were younger. New stuff I didn't understand started happening.

Being bullied on the way to, during, and on the way home from school was one of those new things.

"At times, the taunting and pushing went on for every single step I took."

There were fights on the playground, taunting, pushing, and trash talk. I was really confused. Why did everybody change? What happened? Did I say or do something that made the other kids want to beat me up? Needless to say, I started not liking school. My older brother and sister also got picked on. I often wondered what they did to make those kids mad at them, too.

I guess I was a little slow in figuring it all out, but when I did, it hurt me terribly. Why couldn't we be happy and play like we had before? I tried (in my child's mind) to find a solution, but realized a solution to racial divisions went far beyond my elementary school intellect. I remember knowing inside that what was going on wasn't right. No one told me this, I just knew it. I vowed it would not change me. I wouldn't be like those other kids bullying me. What I still didn't grasp was I had to do what my parents said or else I would get the switch or belt. Here's what I am referring to . . .

When we are little kids, we only know how to BE ourselves. I liked to have fun and explore, just like the other kids. They liked to play with dolls and cars just like I did.

It was what we knew—what we were born with. What changed was what we were taught. The things we heard and saw every day must have taken a few years to sink in. The adults taught us "we" differed from "them". They also cautioned us to never trust (or have anything to do with) "them". Most adults wouldn't allow children to be disrespectful to other adults, so this "us" and "them" were like the clothes we wear beneath our coats. Everyone knows there are clothes under the coat, but no one sees them until the coat comes off.

Being a young kid, I figured my adults had good reasons for telling me this stuff. After all, these same adults taught me how to get dressed, tie my shoes, take a bath, brush my teeth, make my bed, respect adults, and mind my manners. I didn't always like the stuff I had to learn, but it was necessary to become an adult someday. We all learned quickly that if we didn't behave according to the "us and them" training, we would get into trouble.

After things changed, the alleyway behind our house on Marshall Street became the longest road ever! The alley was only two blocks long, but there were days when I didn't think I would make it to the end unscathed. At times, the taunting and pushing went on for every single step I took. On other days, my brother, sister, and I might make it halfway down the alley before some bigger kids would start their bullying again. I'm serious!

Now and then, I would make it all the way to the main street without incident.

When I made it to the end of the alley without incident, I actually thought something was wrong! Were the bullies out sick from school? Did they find someone else to pick on? I admit I thanked God when I could walk to school without being harassed.

Looking back on it now, I doubt the bullying happened every single day. Could it? It sure felt like it did! I would wonder when they were going to tire of it. It seemed they never did. I remember trying to figure out what I did, so I could say I was sorry. For a while, I believed the relentless hate would stop if I apologized.

"This was the only time I've been called a nigger."

Around second or third grade, I finally got it. All the bad words and reasons made sense. It was like all the dots connected, formed the big picture, and I could see it. For me, it was one of those ugly pictures in a coloring book you don't want to waste a crayon on. Unfortunately, this ugly picture had already been "colored in" for me.

My "dots connecting epiphany" didn't sit well with me. Somehow, deep inside, I knew those words, behaviors, and beliefs were not right. How could they be right? Not that they weren't right for me. They simply were not right! I knew it then, and still know it today. That's my truth and I suspect one of the truths.

I think I know what the answer would be if we were to ask Jesus, Buddha, Abraham, the Dalai Lama, or play "pick a sage or prophet for $200".

Once I knew the meaning behind the words, "honky"; "whitey"; "spic"; "dingo"; "nigger"; "chink"; "slant eyes"; "cracker"; and all the rest, I was confused. I didn't understand why I wasn't like my play-friends anymore. That age-defining moment in time separated us forever. Yep, I finally understood all the teasing, hateful words, and bullying had nothing to do with something I did. It had everything to do with the color of my skin . . . the color of everyone's skin. Now how is a seven-year-old supposed to live with that? I wondered if my whole life would be like that alleyway to school. Before long, I found out.

When I was in about the third grade, some government entity closed our once grand elementary school. They created a plan to bus all the neighborhood kids to the West side of town. (At least I think the demolition of our school was why they bussed us. It may have been desegregation as well.) I don't think elementary school children understand desegregation or bussing. We were told we had to ride a bus to our new school across town. And that was that.

The first bus ride to the new school was silent. I guess we all felt a little strange. We were apprehensive because we didn't know what to expect. The bus pulled up in front of the school (somewhere off Evergreen Street).

As soon as we started getting off the bus, I heard taunts like "Go home, niggers!"; "We don't want you here!"; and "Go back to where you came from!". I guess the parents of the students attending that school didn't like the idea of "us" coming to "their" school.

Some white kids got off the bus, and (for a moment) the chants stopped. I guess the taunters expected to just see black kids getting off that bus. It seemed to confuse them a little. Did they really think only black people lived downtown? This was the only time I've been called a nigger. Even though the insult wasn't aimed at me directly, I didn't like it. I could feel the hate spewing out of their mouths. I wondered why they were so mad and didn't want us there. All we needed was a school where we could get our education. Then I remembered the "us" and "them" lesson.

"I've often wondered how different our lives would be . . ."

The kids at this school already knew the difference between "their kind" and "those people". I learned (and was called) another name that year, "nigger lover". That's what they called white kids who were friends with (or hung around) those "other people". We were the ones who stuck up for our neighborhood friends and schoolmates.

At this point, I was disliked by just about everyone except the few kids who had the same belief as me. I was living the old saying, "Can't win for losing."

Amid all this educational doom and gloom, there were some fun times. One of those fun times was making up (and singing) a silly song about the new school we all hated. We would sing it during the bus ride home. I only remember part of the song, but it's permanently etched on my brain . . . "Fart evergreen, shut up!" I think the new school was Evergreen Elementary, but don't hold me to it. What all we were trying to express in that song is beyond me, but I know we couldn't stand that school.

Another fun time for us was the bus ride home. As soon as the last bell rang, we ran as fast as we could to our bus. Everyone was trying to get a seat in the last three or four rows. Our bus went down a road that had a big dip in it. If you were lucky (had a back seat), you'd stand up just before the bus hit the dip and go flying in the air! Every day, our bus driver would tell us to stay seated. Every day we would stand up, fly in the air, and laugh like crazy. The bus driver didn't like us very much. I guess he didn't understand how kids couldn't resist that kind of fun!

Our experience attending the school on Evergreen Street only lasted one or two years. Maybe all those parents protested so much the school board caved to the pressure. I don't know, but the government found another school for us to attend closer to our neighborhood.

Attending this next new school is another of my blank spaces in time. The only proof I went to that school is a newspaper clipping my mom had kept.

The article (written many years later) talked about the school being repurposed. On the clipping, my mom had written a note saying me and my brother had attended school there. I remember not missing the "evergreen school" at all. I was glad I never had to go back! Not long after being reassigned schools again, we moved away from our old neighborhood.

By third grade, the adults had successfully changed the beliefs of their children. Instead of seeing another kid they could laugh and play with, they saw skin color. They now believed they were better than the other kids. Some kids enjoyed this feeling of being better than someone else. I'm guessing since none of us were rich or had a lot, the appeal of belonging or being special was somehow powerful. If you have nothing, at least it's something. Some kids didn't like (or agree with) the racist teachings. They still had to obey their parents or get in trouble. Those kids would act one way around their folks and another at school.

Sometimes we would sneak down the block to play, talk, or laugh again like we used to. We took a chance that no one would see us and snitch. This strategy worked until something happened and racial tensions escalated.

When racial tensions were high, the kids you snuck around with wouldn't even talk to you until things calmed down. One good thing that came from all this craziness was you learned who your real friends were. To be honest, there weren't many.

I've often wondered how different our lives would be if we hadn't been taught all that racist crap and allowed to just be kids. A few kids refused to become racists. They would hang out with whomever they wanted. As I mentioned before, like me, they had it the worst. Not only were their parents on them all the time, but they also alienated everyone else. Basically, if you were friends with someone you weren't supposed to be friends with, both sides came after you.

"I cupped my hand over my mouth and tried not to breathe."

Even though I knew our "training" wasn't right, I also realized I couldn't do anything about it. How can a child in elementary school cure racism? I began staying to myself. That way, I got into less trouble than I otherwise would have. This was the moment in my life when I started to rely on my own company. I started listening more than I talked, observed everything, and learned as much as I could. Somehow, I knew all this would come in handy later on in life.

I remember sneaking into my old elementary school just before it was demolished. They had covered the school with "No Trespassing" signs and boarded-up all the windows. A condemned building was something I'd never experienced. One night, me and my brother went to have a look at our once grand school. We weren't supposed to be at the school. Nor were we supposed to sneak out of the house at night. We certainly didn't want our babysitter to find us missing after she had put us to bed, but what the heck? This was an adventure!

We squeezed in-between the fencing and sheets of plywood to get inside the school. We looked around a bit, but it was empty and dusty. Nothing cool to look at or anything! We decided we'd better get back home before anyone noticed we were missing and we got into big trouble. As we were making ourselves skinny to get through the chain-link fence surrounding the school, a cop car cruised by with their spotlight on! They had made us! We decided within two-seconds to make a break for it. We were more afraid of the butt whippin' we'd get from our mom (if she found out) than we were of anything the cops could do to us.

Let me tell you, we could run! We took off running like the wind! You know that run where you bend your knees and lower your center of gravity? That run where your legs are moving so fast they just look like a blurry circle? (Did you ever watch *The Roadrunner* cartoon?

Remember how the roadrunner's legs turned into a blurry circle every time he took off running?) That night we ran just like the roadrunner speeding away from Wylie Coyote!

We hit the corner and took a sharp right. Then, to confuse the cops, we split up. To catch us both, the cops would have to call in reinforcements! I ran about half a block, then glanced behind me real quick. The spotlight was now close to the corner I had taken just seconds before. I made the split-second decision to leap over this row of hedges close to my house. I figured it was dense enough that the spotlight wouldn't reveal me. And just like that, I was airborne!

I just about cleared the whole hedge, but caught the backside with one of my feet. I ended up on the ground with hedge sticks scratching my back and trying to stick up my bum. Ouch! That hurt. I couldn't yell out or cry. If I did, the cops would hear me! I cupped my hand over my mouth and tried not to breathe. I watched as the spotlight came closer and closer, eventually passing right by my hiding spot! My plan had worked (chuckle)! Once the coast was clear, I headed for my house right down the street. I felt like laughing, but I was too sore. Yeah, stuff like that was harmless and kind of scary fun. It was a relief valve, designed to release the pressure of everyday life. Thank God running from the cops never became my thrill of choice!

You may wonder how long it's been since I lived in the neighborhood. Some people believe if you leave your neighborhood, you forget your roots and how you came up. I don't know about that theory. I do know my behavior has amazed and confused countless people over the years.

Like the times I'd start dancing to "old school" music. Or the few times when some drama popped off and my neck automatically started workin'. Someone disrespected me in a bar once and I immediately started taking off my jewelry before I "went in" (jumped in the fight). A few times, I even jumped in for some double-dutch. These moments are priceless. Yeah, certain things from my formative years will always be a part of me.

"What color were they?"

How we see the world is strongly influenced by what we experience growing up. It drives what we notice, focus on, and the way we run our daily lives. These things never leave you and show up in your life at weird times, catching you off guard like an instinctual autopilot or software running in the background. It happens to me all the time. When my childhood "autopilot" engages, I refer to those events as my having a "black moment".

After about a year of living in Illinois, I decided I wanted to move near mountains like the ones I had seen in Germany.

Snow-covered mountain peaks (like the famous Mt. Fuji in Japan) had always captivated me. My visits to Bavaria (southern Germany) and the cog train ride to the top of The Zugspitz (one of the highest peaks in Germany) cemented my love for the beauty of The Alps. So I set my intent, sold all my belongings, packed my car, and headed to Colorado via Arkansas and Utah. (Yeah, that is a whole other story.)

Once I arrived in Utah, something felt off about the place. I couldn't quite figure out what it was. After a week or two, I still had this weird, nagging feeling. At first, I thought it was because I was in a new place and around different people. The nagging feeling would stay with me until the new school year started. I was in the car with my sister-in-law and she was driving near a school. We passed a little girl walking to school. Suddenly, the answer to what had been causing my weird feeling hit me! I yelled out, "That's it! There's no black people here!" My sister-in-law gave me this look akin to pity, and I seem to recall her saying something about me being a little "slow". So, my experience growing up in the inner city had made my subconscious aware of not seeing any black people. It just hadn't registered in my brain until that moment!

Sometimes my autopilot incidents came in the form of instant anger ("going off"). When this happened, I'd have to stop myself (and calm the heck down) before things got too real and someone called 9-1-1. This anger hit me one day in the break room at work.

Me and a coworker were eating lunch and overheard other staff talking about the good 'ol days. They reminisced about the stores they used to visit downtown. About the soda fountain where they went as children. Nostalgia-type stuff was thick in the air as they recalled the yummy milkshakes, sundaes, and food the soda fountain had served back in the day.

I guess all that talk about the soda fountain triggered a memory for one woman. She said she loved being at the soda fountain on Sunday after church. She talked about sitting there and watching all the "colored women" in beautiful hats come out of the church. I stopped eating and asked my Latina coworker if she had heard what I just heard.

My facial expression must have changed, because my friend looked at me kind of strange and said something about just letting it be. I'm not sure what (or if) I replied to her. I stood up and walked over to the lady who had made the comment. I asked her, "What color were they?"

The lady looked at me like she didn't understand the question, then asked me what I meant. I rephrased the question. "What color were the ladies wearing the hats you were just talking about? Purple, green, blue?" The entire room had gone quiet with a mix of "Oh, shit!" and people holding their breath.

The lady still didn't understand what I was asking her. My friend was probably thinking something was about to pop off. She was trying to get me to come back to our table. I think the other lady eventually said, "Black ladies" but I don't believe she understood what she had said. The whole deal had made my head a little fuzzy.

I took my seat again, and the encounter was over. My friend seemed concerned about someone complaining to management. If anyone did, there might be trouble. I wasn't worried, as I was still hot under the collar about it. Nothing was ever said about the incident.

Stuff like that happens when the time is right for the past to come up and say, "Remember me?" You can count on the past returning from time to time. It's right up there with Murphy's Law. It's important how we handle it when it pops up. I hope the lady in the lunch room never used the term "colored people" again.

"Thank you, Eddie Murphy! Worked like a charm!"

Most of my life has been like that. I'll stand up for someone (or something) and people wonder what the hell kind of dog I have in the fight (being so white and all). Why would a "wonder bread" girl get so angry over the word "colored"? I guess it was because I'd reached my maximum fill level. Enduring stupidity for many years makes a person sick and tired of it.

(By the way, the new term for colored people is "people of color". It's made to sound more palatable, but it's still as negative as its predecessor.) Growing up in black neighborhoods (and learning certain cultural behaviors) would also have a negative impact on my dating life. The one example that stands out above the rest is what I call "My Date with the Sugar Hill Gang".

My blind date and I had enjoyed a nice dinner and conversation. I thought the evening was going well. I felt comfortable with him. After dinner, we got into his truck and an oldies station was playing on the radio. After a few minutes, the song *Rapper's Delight* (short version) by the Sugar Hill Gang came on. It had been ages since I'd heard the song, so I asked my date to turn it up.

Since I felt comfortable with him, I assumed I could be myself. I started singing along with Wonder Mike, Master Gee, and Casanova Fly (Hank). And of course I was dancing in my seat while singing along to that classic tune! I was having a good time, and it made me happy! My date was quiet (and said little) when we pulled up to my car. As we said our goodbyes and thanks, I thought he looked at me differently than he had during our date. I was happy and got into my car, still feeling the giddy effects from my classic rap high.

My date never called again. At first, I didn't understand why. I thought we'd had a good first date.

As I went over the events of that evening, the only possible catalyst for his flip-flop was my joyous sing-a-long to Rapper's Delight. I decided it was okay that he never called back. Who wants a man that doesn't appreciate old-school rap?

As I mentioned earlier, there have been many times in my life when my childhood learning would return to serve me. Other times, it would scare or confuse unsuspecting people. People who threatened me (or tried to make me feel less than they were) experienced it.

My first husband (who liked to get drunk and be abusive) got a good dose of it as well. I admit I often thought of waiting until he passed out, then hitting him repeatedly with an iron skillet. Exacting my payback by dumping hot oatmeal or grits in his lap may have crossed my mind a time or two as well. One day, when I'd had enough, I gave him a cold, dead-eye stare and reminded him he had to sleep sometime. (Thank you, Eddie Murphy! Worked like a charm!)

I remember times when people got in my face instead of talking about whatever had pissed them off. My crazy would come out and my neck would start workin'. The transformation could be quite scary! A normal day would go sideways, and in an instant my hair would go up, jewelry came off, and I'd look for anything made of glass (to protect myself). It wasn't something I thought about or contemplated for days, it just was. I'm telling you, it was an automatic response!

Yeah, all the crazy, deathly quiet stares, neck workin', music, culture stuff would just pop out at the weirdest times. What else could it be except me growing up in a black neighborhood coming out? I knew this stuff wasn't my cracker side! (Chuckle.) Although I've mellowed a great deal as the years have passed, I still have black moments that leave people confused. When I dance, people have said, "You don't dance like a white girl." When I talk about the old school music I like, they usually ask, "What do you know about Luther?" (Luther Vandross was an iconic R&B singer.)

Growing up in black neighborhoods came to the forefront when I returned home after twenty-something years. While working as a trainer, my students would constantly ask me where I was from. When I told them I was from Arkansas, they didn't believe me! Some days I'd make a game of it and give a prize to the first student who could correctly guess what state I was from. (This made the class fun, and the time would go by faster.)

Some students who seemed to want to disprove my claim would ask me follow-up questions. One such question was what part of town I grew up in. When I told them downtown, Rose City, and southwest, (all inner-city "hoods") they looked at me with confused expressions. Another popular debunking question was which high school I graduated from. When I responded with "Mc-Clellan," I think it chipped away at their initial disbelief.

Perhaps they didn't believe I was a native because I had lost my accent. I know part of it was because the color of my skin didn't match the areas I grew up in. Sometimes I would share with my students some of the street names I grew up on just to watch the expressions on their faces change! Hey, I'm a closet comedian! I try to find humor in life. Spending years living in different countries and speaking their languages must have caused my losing my home state accent. It's still funny that people want proof that Arkansas is really my home state!

What Growing Up "Black" Taught Me

1. Children aren't born racist. We teach children racism. People of any race can be racist and experience racism.
2. Racism comes from the ego self. It's a belief that one person is better than another because of the color of their skin.
3. Dr. Martin Luther King, Jr. was right about not judging a man by the color of his skin, but the content of his character.
4. The culture, language, and experiences we have in childhood never leaves us. We are a patchwork quilt of all the stuff we took in. When the time is right, the past pops up in our life (reminding us we need to address it).

5. We are the total of all our learning and experience. Hopefully, we learn to recognize which parts serve our highest good and which do not. Our lives are so much better when we release the parts that cause us drama or instant anger.

6. Love and respect are always be more powerful than hate and discord.

7. Taking responsibility for your own actions and not blaming others for your situation in life will lift you higher than any amount of money or position you may hold.

8. If we want to end racism, all we have to do is stop teaching it to our children, stop reinforcing it in our schools, and stop allowing our governments to sow division between people.

Who? . . . I
What? . . . Walk the Red Road
When? . . . All the days of my life
Where? . . . Wherever I may go in my life
Why? . . . For The People, because my heart is Red.

3
Cowboys and Indians

It seems it wasn't long after we started going to the other school closer to home that my mom and dad split up. I guess my mom had finally had enough of the drunken fights and abuse from my dad. After the cops came and took him away, my mom moved us away from the downtown neighborhood where I had spent my formative years. First, she rented a house in an area of town called Rose City. We lived there for a couple of years before moving to an area called "southwest".

Exactly where we lived (and when we lived there) remains tangled up (like a string of Christmas tree lights) in my mind. We moved about seven or eight times over the same number of years! I remember starting sixth grade at Baseline Elementary, so our first place to live on that side of town must have been American Manor. It was there I discovered a new running game called "Cowboys and Indians". Instead of running from the cops, I started running through the woods.

Not long after we'd moved to our new place, we found out from the local kids about the woods where everybody played. Turns out, the woods were close by and the "in" place to be. The neighborhood kids spent a great deal of time in those woods. Back then, parents still let their kids go outside and play without supervision.

We played a lot of games in those woods (like hide-n-seek, chase, and cowboys and Indians) even after we moved to the house on Pine Cone Drive. I liked cowboys and Indians the best. Some kids would play the cowboys and others the Indians. The Indians would run into the woods and hide. Then the cowboys would try to hunt them down. We mostly made up the rules of the game as we went along. Young people are creative like that.

This game concept must have come from watching those "spaghetti western" type movies. Except for Tonto in *The Lone Ranger* series, they portrayed movie Indians as bad guys. The cowboys (or soldiers) they always depicted as good guys. The good guys constantly chased or hunted down the "bad" Indians. There was always some big Indian war party circling the poor settler's wagons and gunfights to the death.

In this game, I always wanted to play the Indian. I really didn't like the cowboys or soldiers. I remember I could run through the woods really fast, zigzag around logs, jump over bushes, and climb like crazy. Guess I was quite the tomboy back then. I could hide behind a tree and the "cowboys" would walk right past me.

Sometimes I hid so well the other kids would give up looking for me and go home.

People may think these feats of physical prowess were just my kid's imagination at work. Maybe I didn't run as fast as the wind. Perhaps I couldn't just disappear behind a tree. All I know is, something planted solidly these memories in my brain. Running, hiding, or playing in the woods made me feel like a real Indian! I didn't fear the forest because I talked to the trees and animals. The woods were my friends. I think all children like animals, trees, flowers, gardens, and other stuff when they're little. It seems things we were taught; accepted as truth; and our traumatic experiences make us afraid of nature.

During my "playing Indian" time, I hadn't yet realized how pale my skin was without a tan. Believing I was an Indian came from the inside. I seem to remember telling other kids I was an Indian, but I eventually stopped doing that. Why would a pale, blue-eyed white girl think she was an Indian? My hair was blonde during these years, so that didn't help matters either.

To be honest, I think it planted itself in my brain for a couple of reasons. First, I had heard relatives from both sides of my family mention we had Cherokee, Sioux, and Apache blood. It's stuff I picked up from listening to the adult conversations going on around me growing up. That's what I believed happened. When I look back now, I think those names came from the whispers of relatives and those cowboy movies we watched as kids.

Second, I related more to the Indians than the cowboys. I can't tell you why. It was something I felt inside. When I watched those movies, I usually felt sorry for the Indians. It didn't seem like they got a fair deal most of the time. I actually thought I understood why they acted the way they did (although I probably couldn't have explained it at the time). So maybe my connection to them made me pay attention to the names in the movies. Who can say for sure?

"I thought the whole thing was a cover-up to fit what our civilization expected."

My exciting days of playing the Indian and running through the woods ended after we moved to Jamestown Apartments. When we were young, we walked everywhere. Unfortunately, our new apartment was too far away from our beloved woods to visit.

At that time, I was attending Cloverdale Junior High School and getting a little too old to play games with the younger kids anymore. I hung on to the belief of being part Indian, though. I didn't talk about it much, except to my siblings. At some point, I realized I didn't look like other real Indians. Turns out, they filled those spaghetti westerns with white actors in makeup and "war paint".

Glancing back in time, the western movies probably mentioned those Indian nations a lot because the public was familiar with them.

Having studied Native American history as an adult, I surmise the odds of two parents having the lineage of these three distinct nations as slim. (My understanding of the areas where these nations lived.) To get a professional opinion of my theory, a cultural anthropologist or oral historian from each nation needs to be consulted.

Regardless, I've carried the belief of being Indian inside me all my life. Occasionally (as I grew older), I would ask relatives about it. None of them seemed inclined to discuss this side of our heritage. I could see there were no living relatives that displayed any Indian dress, customs, stories, etc. I thought the whole thing was a cover-up to fit what our civilization expected. Being anything other than white during my parents' and grandparents' time was not safe. That was the general vibe I got from asking "Indian questions".

Many years later, I asked my mom about it again. Maybe enough time had passed, but she told me she remembered Cree and Creek being part of our heritage. Although this made more sense to me (later on), I was really shocked not to hear Cherokee, Sioux, or Apache. My mom told me she knew nothing about those other nations and wondered how I'd gotten that into my head.

One of my aunts was into researching our family tree. She had a knack for digging up historical documents. She also had first-hand knowledge of our relatives. One day, she told me our family did indeed have Indian bloodlines.

She revealed that my great-grandmother was a full-blood Seminole.

Now I was really confused! These Indian nations were lining up faster than I could sort them in my mind. I had seen pictures of my great-grandmother and she was not pasty white like me. She actually looked like an Indian! Since my mom's parents were from Alabama/Georgia, the Seminole connection wasn't that far-fetched in my mind. I had learned a lot about the geographical areas of the North American nations by then. The Seminole were mostly in Florida, so south Georgia/Alabama was plausible.

"We stayed away so long we never made friends with the woods again."

Still, the curiosity about my Indian heritage from either side of the family remained. I was at the point in my learning where I was a sponge, soaking up information and storing it in my vast complex of brain cells. Memories of my childhood beliefs about my "Indian connection" compelled me to set about trying to prove it. I had no particular reason other than to answer the identity questions I had growing up.

I thought that belonging to an Indian nation would give me an identity that matched what I felt inside. It would help me feel a part of this crazy civilization. I guess you might call it a soul search.

After learning the Seminole information in my late twenties, I doubted the accuracy of this latest tidbit of information. Nobody talking about it for so long is what made me skeptical.

People would give me funny looks when I said I was an Indian. Some said, "Let me guess . . . Cherokee, right?" like it was a joke. I didn't think it was funny! Most of my life, I felt like an Indian on the inside and a real white girl on the outside. This identity crisis made me feel even more like an outsider.

Time passed, and for about fifteen years, I forgot about my Indian side. I was busy finishing high school and starting my first career. I got married and thought I'd have a family (what they expected of little girls once they became women). As children, we are told fairy tales about how life turns out. It doesn't always end in "happily ever after". This was one of my life lessons.

When I think back on my young Indian life, I don't remember being afraid of the woods. (Maybe because I had developed a "country side" from spending time with my grandparents.) I'm pretty sure fear came later as I learned about people who would kidnap, sexually assault, and even kill kids. The woods became a strange and scary place where I wasn't allowed to go anymore. Once beautiful trees disappeared so developers could build houses and businesses. Once small children became teenagers and discovered other stuff to do.

Yep, we didn't realize it at the time, but the scary stories, warnings, and getting older kept us away. We stayed away so long we never made friends with the woods again. Although it was many years later, I eventually made friends with the trees again when I became a spiritual seeker.

NOTE: While revising this book, I read the Seminole primarily came from the Creek Indians who had moved into Florida from southern Georgia and Alabama. (This was during the time Spain owned Florida.) They allegedly intermingled with African-American slaves, whom had escaped captivity and the Muskogee (or Muscogee) Nation. Other historical sites say the Seminole were indigenous to Florida and didn't migrate. According to others, there had been trouble between the Creek and the Seminole and they made an agreement on where they'd settle. So, regardless of the conflicting "historical" accounts of the Seminole, the tidbits my aunt and mother shared with me finally makes sense.

What Being an "Indian" Taught Me

1. Sometimes we feel a kinship with other cultures. This is our heart and soul whispering to us. We should pay attention.
2. We are part of the land. The land sustains us. We should do our best to preserve and protect it.

3. Oxygen and sunshine are essential to our health. We should go outdoors and enjoy them as much as possible.

4. It's not always about your lineage or the culture you grew up in. It's about what feels right inside.

5. I'm a white woman who has a Native American center. I will always be this way, and it's okay!

One of those days I had to do something I'd rather not.

Sitting in court for bankruptcy, thinking how poor I was.
Hearing a voice say, "You're not poor!"

Crying my eyes out.

Realizing though I have nothing in the material sense, I have so much more.

Feeling I was given a gift . . . a most precious one.

Because I knew it to be the truth.

4
Growing Up Poor

How did I know my family was poor? It wasn't because I was aware of some government poverty guidelines that told me we were poor. I knew we were poor based on stuff that went on in our everyday lives. When you're poor, you have little to make you feel good about your circumstance except family and good times. The holiday and birthday meals shared with family, and the occasional family reunion, could make you feel rich!

It seems strange, but poor people would differentiate themselves from other poor people. I never really understood why. Wouldn't it have been better to stick together (like a family)? Instead, they acted like they were better than other poor people. Maybe it helped them feel better about themselves because they weren't as destitute as others. I don't know for sure. It just seemed ridiculous to me.

There was a poor scale of sorts: poor (just poor); dirt poor (didn't have two nickels to rub together); didn't have a pot to piss in (guess that's self-explanatory); and something like destitute (homeless, living on the street, couch surfing, or something similar). I think they're listed in order from least to most poor . . . as if there could be such a thing.

Being poor bothered some of my siblings more than others. After a while, you get used to being poor. It's not like you have a choice. Sometimes you get fed up with being told you don't have money. We tested two methods to see which worked better. First, we simply stopped asking for anything. Second, we kept asking, hoping for a yes now and then. We determined both worked equally well. Ninety percent of the time, we still didn't get whatever we'd asked for. We also learned reverse psychology (not asking) didn't work on softening up our mom.

"Childhood taste buds don't lie!"

Being poor causes a high level of embarrassment and cruel teasing by other kids who didn't learn (or didn't use) manners. My brothers and sisters may have been moneyless, but mom taught us manners and respect. She expected us to practice both every single minute of our waking hours. To break manner or respect rules was an automatic butt whippin', usually beginning with having to pick our own switch from the bush in the backyard.

If we picked a wimpy switch, our mom would send us back to pick two! (Then she would wear them both out on our backsides.) Obviously, having to pick my instrument of punishment was not fun, but it taught me valuable lessons. One is to take responsibility for your actions and their consequences.

When you're poor, you learn how to stretch a dollar. You also learn tricks to make everything you buy go a little further or last a little longer. This works okay for most things, like adding a little water to laundry soap; mixing nonfat dry milk and water with real milk, and using coffee grounds twice. Buying groceries like flour, potatoes, rice, cornmeal, and beans (that fill hungry bellies) also works well. As helpful as all those tricks were, I didn't like it when my mom used similar strategies for the occasional treats!

We didn't get treats often, but if they were on sale when mom went to the Hostess Bakery Store, she would bring some home. We had to share them to make them last a little longer. Each sibling could have one Twinkie or Suzy Q (from a two-pack), half a fruit pie, or one Ding Dong. It was like torture! Why we couldn't have our own individual package? I took a liking to Ding Dongs because I didn't have to share. I was SO glad they had individual foil wrapping! Happy day! I could enjoy the whole thing! It was a small treat, but it was all mine!

Mom would tell us we could only have one treat a day. Sometimes we would conspire to share an extra one.

Other times, we would sneak an extra one for ourselves and hope we didn't get busted by one of our siblings. If one of them caught us, we would have to promise something in return for their silence. Yeah, it seems children learn the art of blackmail early on. Unfortunately, the promised silence usually only lasted until said brother or sister was in hot water over something. Then they would turn into a snitch, hoping to reduce the severity of their own punishment. Having so many siblings was hard on the keeping secrets business. There were so many remembered stories and details that once the snitching started, it was like a round-robin purging of personal wrongs committed by several parties.

Somehow, our mom always knew if we had eaten any extra snacks. I often wondered if she counted them before she left for work. Sometimes I believed she had some kind of "spidey sense" about anything we had done and tried to hide. As a child, I believed my mom could look at the Twinkie box and know it was one or two short!

Most of the time, we didn't get an allowance (spending money). Occasionally, we might find some cash in our birthday cards or maybe the tooth fairy would pay us a visit. Mom expected us to keep our rooms clean without pay. Kids today might view this as some kind of punishment. For me, spending money came mostly from cashing in soda bottles and catching moths.

Making a little extra pocket change was like having a job.

I walked around the neighborhood looking for pop bottles (I think they were worth five cents each). Some days, I found as many bottles as I could carry, and others I'd find only one or two. I also caught moths for our next-door neighbor for a few cents each. He was an old man and hated moths because they got into his garden.

All the neighborhood kids traded in their soda bottles at the corner store. We used the money to buy awesome candy like Jolly Ranchers, Chik-O-Sticks, Super Bubble bubblegum, and Now or Laters. My favorite Jolly Rancher flavor was apple. I'm not sure why, but it was the best flavor ever! Watermelon was my favorite flavor of Now or Later. Their green apple was good, but not as good as the Jolly Rancher apple. If I had a good bottle day (or turned over enough moth bodies to the old man), I would have enough money to buy a Zero, Pay Day, or Baby Ruth candy bar. Sometimes I would get snacks like a Hostess Apple Pie, Twinkies, or Suzy Q's just so I could have the whole thing to myself.

Sweets tasted better back in the day (before they started using chemicals and artificial this and that). I'm just sayin'. Did you know a certain golden sponge cake (and others) used to have real cream filling in the middle? Seriously! Look at some old snack box photos (the ingredients list) and you'll see what I'm talking about.

These days that cream filling is called "creamy filling". The real chocolate is now labeled "chocolatey".

I guess "creamy" means consistency versus ingredient and "chocolatey" means something that simulates the taste of chocolate. The fresh and yummy treats I remember from childhood now have twenty or more ingredients. Yes, my friend, there is a big difference! Childhood taste buds don't lie!

It's a sad truth that the snacks from the old days are now just a batch of chemicals, artificial flavors and colors, GMOs, sugar, and preservatives. Ick! I guess in a way it's a good thing those tasty treats stopped being tasty to me. Had they maintained their awesome yumminess, I might have become an enormous woman!

During the summer months, we wanted ice cream. Any old ice cream wouldn't do. It had to be a frozen treat from the neighborhood ice cream man. Does anyone remember orange cream popsicles, fudge bars, ice cream sandwiches, or nutty cones? What about the red, white, and blue fat popsicle called "The Bomb"? (I'm salivating just thinking about it!) We didn't get these special treats very often, but when we did, it was awesome!

One of the best things about being a kid was eating ice cream! Nothing cools you down from the summer heat better than a frosty treat! The moment I heard the ice cream man's music, I would run to my mom and beg her for some money, bouncing up and down excitedly! Sometimes I wanted nothing more in the world than that ice cream! I just knew I would die if I didn't get any!

But just like the snack cakes, they started making ice cream treats with cheaper ingredients and loads of chemicals.

"Wearing homemade clothes was like being chum thrown into the water to attract sharks."

If you've never experienced the pandemonium that ensues with a visit from the ice cream man, watch Eddie Murphy's comedy special *Delirious.* I remember the first time I watched his special. I laughed so hard my stomach was hurting and I was crying. It was just like I remember growing up. My mom used to make us "better than McDonald's" burgers too! (If you do not know what I'm talking about, spend a couple bucks and watch that classic comedy special.)

Alas, my moth-catching job didn't last long. At some point, I realized I was being paid less than the fair market rate for catching those flittering tricksters. So, I started reselling dead moths back to the old man. Eventually, he caught on to my scheme and didn't require my services any longer. Worse yet, he told my mom what I'd been doing! This didn't bother me, as I saw him as a two-faced, racist hypocrite. He was mean and didn't like kids, anyway. He was one of those types who made the kids' daily lives hard.

When we moved to our new neighborhood, pop bottles were hard to find. Side jobs for pocket money were few and far between. It was back to sharing Hostess snack cakes and longing for the ice cream man. I learned to deal with pretty much all the "don't have two pennies to rub together" stuff except one. I experienced acute anxiety over handmade clothes. My mom knew how to sew, but somehow other kids just knew if your clothes weren't "store bought". The kids I went to school with could be viciously cruel. Wearing homemade clothes was like being chum thrown into the water to attract sharks. Believe me, it didn't take long for the bullies to circle.

The one outfit I remember most was a Pep Club uniform. It seemed the other girls bought their uniforms from the uniform store (like for cheerleaders). Mom made my uniform with a sewing machine at home. I absolutely dreaded going to that first football game in my sewn skirt, Goodwill white shirt, white Ked-like tennis shoes, and white socks that weren't the right length. I was so self-conscious I wanted to die or shrivel up in a dark corner somewhere (partly because of oncoming hormone changes, I'm sure).

Some of the Pep Club students just gave me a "poor you" look. Others made remarks I no longer remember. I remember not wanting to go to another game ever! Yeah, maybe a lot of it was my being self-conscious, but soon after I stopped trying to take part in public extracurricular activities.

I was much more comfortable with the more introverted Chess Club, Spanish Club, and Band. Before high school was over, I became part of the outcast or stoner group.

I don't remember handmade clothes after that year. I am not sure why. Maybe we just stuck with hand-me-downs, Goodwill, Salvation Army, or yard sales. Don't think I'm being a whiner! These experiences taught me a lot. I learned to be grateful, work hard, and appreciate my accomplishments. Looking back now, I realize I probably made my mom feel inadequate. It's funny how we see things clear as day when we get older.

"After all, I had been there . . . done that."

Mom did the best she could do, being a single mom raising a big family. I bet she put a lot of love into those clothes she made for us on her sewing machine. Back then, I couldn't see it or appreciate it. Years pass, things change, and you lose the people that brought you up. It's then when you see the sacrifice and hardship they endured for you and others, but that story is yet to be told.

The worst part about being poor for me was other kids (and sometimes adults) making fun or making condescending remarks. Now that I'm an adult, I know they did it to make themselves feel better or to make up for something missing in their lives. I hope I gave them some healing in that way.

I could understand harsh words or looks if I was doing something that was my fault, but how was being poor my fault?

I believed being poor fit in the same category as the color of my skin. Neither had to do with anything within my control. The Creator made us in his own image. Others ridiculed that goodness and perfection. We have no control over the color of our skin, the financial situation of our parents, and so much more that makes us unique. Our uniqueness doesn't make us less than others. The people doing the judging and ridiculing were turning their noses up at one of God's creations! I guess they didn't think about being one of God's creations too! I never understood that. My brain has always worked this way. I've always sought clarification on things that made little sense or were illogical.

Growing up poor gave me the strength and motivation to be more . . . to have more. It led me to take risks others might see as significant risks or crazy. The risks assisted me in becoming a good helper of others less fortunate. I didn't do good deeds because I needed the credit, expected praise, or because it was the "in" thing to do. My good deeds came from understanding and empathy for others. I understood their situation. After all, I had been there . . . done that.

I've always wanted to share my insights to help others overcome whatever has plagued them for a while or a lifetime.

People have said to me, "You're not an alcoholic. How would you know?" They don't see what I've experienced. They only see the outside. Being born with money wouldn't have changed the outcome (I don't think). I would still help because it's a soul thing. It is me and I am it. If given the choice to go back and change my growing up circumstances with money, I wouldn't do it. Why, you may ask? Because I believe it's an integral part of what made me who I am today.

There are reasons for everything. I didn't understand the purpose of being poor until I was mature enough to understand it. It was the evolution of perfection in the making. All that I've learned and experienced has made me uniquely qualified to do what I came here to do. Why would I want to change anything?

What Being Poor Taught Me

1. Don't judge people who have more (or less) money or possessions than you.
2. We don't know the damage we can do to others with our words, thoughts, actions, or looks. Choose them wisely.
3. Anytime we think we are better than someone else, we dehumanize them.
4. Viewing people as less than others brings about prejudice, racism, and many negatives that plagues society.

5. Those who have more should give more. Everyone can give of their time, talent, or treasure.
6. Those born into poverty should do their best to lift themselves up instead of blaming others or society.
7. Remember where you came from (and where you've been). Use the lessons you learned to live a better life.
8. Don't forget to give yourself a treat now and then. Relish it greatly!
9. Only you can change you or your circumstance.

*And so we strive to be that which is expected,
yet never do we see ourselves in reflections.*

*The circle has come around again and we wonder at
the answer
to what seems so unobtainable.*

*If only we could see it does not lie without.
Wisdom, love, and self do lie <u>Within</u>.*

5
Street Smart and Country Wise

Talk about having an identity crisis . . . not only did I learn black, Indian, and white stuff, I also learned how to live in the city and country. I saw myself as this big 'ol pot of gumbo simmering on the stove, with more ingredients being thrown in as time passed. My parents lived in the city where I spent most of my time growing up. Summer and school breaks I spent working on my grandparent's farm.

In the city I learned to: Ride a bus; watch my back; look both ways before I crossed the street; find the best hiding spots; skip school without getting caught; and take alleyways or shortcuts to avoid detection. Other cultural tidbits included being careful around the police and not being a snitch. Two automatic rules were to run like hell when shit just happens out of nowhere, and avoid fights you know you can't win by acting crazy.

Crazy, now there's a word open to interpretation. I figured out that nobody wants to fight a crazy person and everybody has a built-in "crazy alarm". Some people's alarm goes off if you just start laughing and don't stop. This is especially true if it's not a regular laugh, but an angry-mixed-with-losing-your-mind kind of laugh (something close to the Vincent Price laugh at the end of *Thriller*). Other people's crazy alarm went off if you looked at them with big eyes (like you were about to explode and couldn't wait to whip that ass). With the skittish kids, you could stare right through them, not flinch a muscle, and put on your "make my day" face. Sometimes quiet was the best weapon to scare your opponent.

"Nothing could get my blood boiling quicker than someone picking on my brother."

Believe it or not, people get those vibes you send out. If I knew the kid had a reputation for winning a lot of fights (was a bad-ass) and had set their sights on me for whatever reason, I just went "full-on" crazy. Yep, FULL-ON! Full-on is when you throw all your crazies together and scare your opponent enough that they change their mind about fighting you at all. In full-on, you refer to yourself in the third person, make weird noises, hit yourself, or hold your head like it's about ready to explode. Talking crazy is mandatory in these situations.

Crazy talk is a mixture of gibberish and actual words designed to convince your opponent that you don't care and have nothing to lose. It may even make them think you actually enjoy inflicting pain and suffering. Girls who don't want to risk their good looks will not fight a crazy girl.

In the city, I got picked on for many reasons. My skin was white, I wore glasses, had an eye defect, didn't have money, wasn't pretty, and had poor posture. Sometimes it was when something racial had happened and tensions were high. Everyone chose a side in those times, and it seemed to me I couldn't win no matter which side I picked. Inside, I wanted to pick whomever was in the right. That's what my built-in instincts told me to do.

In all honesty, I learned that if I didn't choose "us" I was in deep shit on the home front. So, I kept my mouth shut and didn't choose sides. This caused me grief, but not as much grief had I picked a side. Of course, both sides believed they were right. Everyone thought they were right for various reasons. They couldn't fathom the possibility that both sides could be right.

There were other times I got into it protecting my younger brother. He was born with physical problems and the kids would pick on him without mercy. In those days, nothing could get my blood boiling quicker than someone picking on my brother. Other times I got into fights because I looked at someone the wrong way. Or maybe I looked at them too long.

Maybe I was in the wrong place at the wrong time. Basically, people picked any reason to get offended in the inner city. There were times I didn't even realize something had happened until stuff instantly went sideways.

Growing up in the city, I learned all the lessons of minding my business; always watching my surroundings; only walking certain ways home from school; not trash-talking anyone; and not staring at anyone. I also learned (in case of a fight) to tie my hair back, take off any jewelry, and find something close to defend myself with. This was usually a Mad Dog 20/20, Boones Farm Strawberry Hill, or soda bottle smashed on the curb, so it had lots of jagged edges. If you knew ahead of time a fight was on, you could also rub a little baby oil on your skin. That way, it would be hard for anyone to get a good grip on you.

"I could shoot a rabbit on the run, or a squirrel going in circles around a tree trunk."

One of the HUGE lessons learned in the hood was you could play "Your mama so fat . . . " with your best friends, but never talk about somebody's momma for real. Doing that will get you an ass-kickin' quicker than most anything else. I did it once . . . once! To this day I remember that lesson because a boy hit me square in my jaw and I saw stars for a few minutes.

My mom spent almost thirty years of her life living off Camp Robinson in Levy (another inner city hood). Although we lived in some challenging areas growing up, I think all my sisters and brothers couldn't wait for summer or spring break so we could go to grandma and grandpa's house. Being on their farm was like being on vacation from the daily city grind.

Grandma and grandpa had lots of land (160 acres). They were simple farmers who usually planted soybeans or rice. They had cows, pigs, dogs, a horse, a donkey, chickens, and guinea hens. There were deer, ducks, squirrels, and rabbits everywhere. We also had run-ins with snakes like garters, copperheads, water moccasins, rattlesnakes, and blue racers. The kids learned early on which snakes were good and bad. When grandpa and grandma took off the head of a venomous snake, they seemed fearless. Grandpa would keep "trophy rattles" from the bigger rattlesnakes he killed. They made for a good story to tell when neighbors would stop by and visit. I remember one rattle had thirteen rattles on it! That was an enormous snake. Snakes really didn't scare me because I respected them and knew how to watch out for them.

As a kid, I traveled all over those acres and acres of woods. I would take a cane pole (with some line, bobber, sinker, and hook) to fish the stream that ran through part of the property. Fresh, dug-up worms were my high-tech fishing bait.

No fancy lures, spinners, or glow-in-the-dark fake bait. It seemed like all the fish I caught liked worms just fine. They were juicy and moved around . . . at least for a short while.

In the country, I also learned to hunt wild game. My grandpa had several rifles with stocks he'd carved himself. My brother used the bigger guns, while I mostly used a .22 rifle. The .22 was small, didn't kick my butt with its recoil, and the shot didn't ruin the meat. I could shoot a rabbit on the run, or a squirrel going in circles around a tree trunk.

Pulling a rabbit out of a hollow in a tree was easy-peasy as well. We never hunted for sport. The wild animals or livestock we killed were for food. My grandparents had little money and the tiny corner store with just essentials was miles away. A real grocery store was 30-40 miles away. So they mostly lived off the land.

There was an orchard in the backyard with Granny Smith and Golden Delicious apples, peaches, and persimmons. Grandma would plant a sizeable garden every year. In the summer and fall, we spent a lot of time shucking corn, stringing beans, popping purple hull peas, and chopping up veggies for canning.

She canned everything under the sun. I learned to plant a garden, weed it, water it, cook, and can. I also learned how to build fires in the wood stoves. The wood stoves were the only source of heat and cooking for the house.

Speaking of cooking, I fondly remember some of the food my grandma used to cook. It still makes my mouth water to this day! Like smelling the fresh bread, baking and eating a still-warm slice with lots of butter! She could cook up some mean fried chicken and rabbit with gravy! I didn't like squirrel meat or duck. The squirrel had a lot of muscle, and the duck tasted gamey.

"Some nights were really dark and creepy, and every sound made you jump."

One of my favorite sides was fresh green beans fried in bacon grease. I'm not sure what spices grandma used, but those were the best green beans ever! I haven't been able to recreate the exact smells and tastes of my grandma's cooking. Sometimes I close my eyes and remember the smell of the cookstove and the delicious food that came from it.

To pass the bit of free time I'd have after all the chores were done, I read back issues of Reader's Digest. My grandma loved *Reader's Digest*, and it seemed she had kept every issue she'd ever received. Grandpa had made a bookshelf that covered an entire wall, and it was full of back issues dating from the late 1950s. Grandma kept those issues because she loved to read and I did too!

Those back issues made life seem cool and less stressed back then. My favorite section was *Word Power* (I think it was called something else before).

I completed just about every English word definition challenge in the entire issue collection! I was a smart kid. That two-page learning tool in "The Digest" could have helped me become a Spelling Bee champion if things had been different.

Besides reading, my other favorite pastime (especially in the winter) was sitting near the fired-up wood stove, rocking in a handmade rocking chair, and singing for my grandma while she cooked in the kitchen. Grandma was a believer and didn't get to go to church often, so I guess my singing was kind of like hearing the choir during Sunday service. I'd learned lots of hymns from singing in the choir of the various churches I'd been kicked out of. My grandma always enjoyed listening to me sing and told me what a beautiful voice I had. I would sing those hymns to her and also patriotic songs like *The National Anthem* or *America the Beautiful*. Now I don't know if I truly had a beautiful voice. Maybe my grandma believed all voices lifted to glorify God were perfect, but she always made me feel like I wanted to keep on singing!

After putting in long hours in the garden, taking care of the animals, or playing hard, we would put in more work to take a bath. We'd build a fire, pump water from the well to fill a washtub, then set the tub over the fire to heat the water (their little log cabin didn't have a bathroom). Once the water was hot, we took the tub off the fire and hid behind some strung-up sheets to take a bath. Grandma caught rainwater for us to wash our hair.

She told us well water was too "hard" for hair. Finally, we would be ready to settle down and go to bed.

I remember the wrought-iron bed, goose-down pillows, and hand-sewn quilts put me to sleep real quick. I always hoped I would sleep through the night. Getting up in the middle of the night to use the bathroom was spooky. In the summer, we had to grab the flashlight, put on our shoes and robe, and walk to the outhouse. Some nights were really dark and creepy, and every sound made you jump. In the winter, we had a coffee can in the bedroom's corner to use. I hated using it. Guess our grandparents didn't want us going outside, getting too cold, then becoming sick.

Over time, I learned every nook and cranny of those 160 acres. I knew right where the muscadine vines grew each year and the best blackberry bush locations. Let me tell you, those blackberry bushes don't give up their sweetness without a fight! Between the heat, the "skeeters", and the thorns, I'd come back with scratches all over my legs and arms. The scratches itched like crazy. My suffering was worth it when my grandma would make me blackberry pie or jam.

"Living a life surrounded by lies is servitude."

Yeah, I played Indian in those woods too. There were times when I took playing Indian a bit too far.

Sometimes I'd disappear into the trees for a while or track my brother when he was out hunting. At one point, I decided I didn't want to use the big Western saddle on Ginger (the horse) when I rode her. I felt sorry for her having to carry all that weight plus me. Since I had become an excellent horsewoman, I got my way (sometimes) and didn't have to use the saddle. At those times, I could use just the horse blanket. Using just a blanket made me happy, and I felt more Indian that way.

I remember one day I got it into my head that I wanted to ride without the bridle and reins. I pictured myself guiding Ginger by gently tugging her mane left or right while pressing my heel into the same flank. Just to try out my theory, I talked my brother into taking the reins off while I was still on the horse.

Well, I had forgotten one tiny detail in all my smartness and eagerness to be a complete Indian. Ginger always broke into a run, running like a wild horse set free once we took the bridle off her. She was smart enough to know it meant we'd finished riding (torturing) her for the day.

It didn't take Ginger long to give me my "should have known better" lesson. As soon as my brother slipped the reins and bit off, Ginger bolted into a full gallop! She made one quick turn around a sticker bush and dumped me into it! Man, did that hurt! So much for my plans to become a completed Indian.

I gave my grandparents one heck of a scare that day! Once they realized I was okay, I got into a heap of trouble. I was lucky that day. I could have been seriously hurt or killed. Alas, I gave up on my dream of riding a horse without a bridle and reins that day.

Besides the skills of riding and caring for a horse, I learned how to milk cows on the farm. I don't think I was very good at it. I had a hard time trying to get the milk to come out of the teat. When it did, it sprayed just about everywhere except into the milk bucket. Bless my grandma's heart . . . she was patient with me.

In mastering how to tend to cows, I figured out you have to be careful where you let your cows graze. Sometimes they'll eat something and it shows up in the milk. I remember taking a drink of milk after milking one day and my mouth shriveled up from the bitter taste! I spit the milk out and told Grandma. She smelled it and said, "Yep, cows been in them bitter weeds again."

The hardest part of raising cows is when it's time to send them off to slaughter. This is especially true if you've attached yourself to a baby cow and watched it grow. So, I learned to respect cows but not get too close to them. It didn't always work, but I understood we had to eat and make a living, so that was that.

Knowing what I do about what cows eat and what it does to their milk almost immediately, you can't tell me the hormones, GMO feed, and whatever else they're fed these days is safe for the milk or meat we consume.

People who haven't spent time around cows aren't aware of stuff like that. I learned some things growing up that have stuck with me, so I'm not so easily fooled by what the media and big corporations try to sell us.

At some point, the people who know how to farm and ranch will be gone. The ones left won't know any better and won't do research to find the answers. The thought of that is just sad. I plan on doing my part to educate people so they can pass it on to other people so we don't forget. Knowing the truth is real freedom. Living a life surrounded by lies is servitude.

Like cows, I learned how to take care of pigs and chickens too. The pigs were dirty and would eat anything, so I cared little for them. I know that's just how they are, but it was a smelly business. I thought the baby pigs were cute until they became adults. Like cows, pigs were raised and fattened up until it was time to sell them. One pig would provide enough meat to make it through the winter.

Raising chickens was my favorite livestock job. I loved seeing the baby chicks following their moms around the yard. They were so fuzzy and cute and had the most adorable voices! One time, the baby chicks got caught outside in a fierce thunderstorm. We tried rescuing a few by wrapping them in towels and putting them in the oven to warm up. Several of them didn't make it.

I cried because they were so young and didn't stand a chance against that early spring storm. I adopted a little black chick survivor that day and gave it a name. My little chick was lucky. He survived the storm and grew up to be a rooster! He would never become part of the family dinner.

"The beautiful and green had become sick and barren, much like the landscape of my heart."

By doing all that stuff around the farm, I guess you could say I was pretty big for my britches. When I was young (nine or ten), I drove a red and white Massey Ferguson tractor. I also fed livestock, picked fruit, tended the garden, built fires, and helped with dressing meat. A person has to be multi-skilled to live on a farm.

I could climb a tree real quick and stay up there for a while. I liked the trees, and they were one of my favorite hiding spots. My brother could walk right past me and never know I was there. I'd also hide up in a tree when I was in big trouble with grandpa. He'd be looking for me to give me my whippin' and I'd hide in a tree. Eventually, I'd get my courage up and come down to take my medicine. It was a hard pill to swallow because grandpa had a razor strop he used as a belt. If I got him all worked up by misbehaving, the licks wouldn't be easy.

It's funny how when you're a kid, you know the moment you've broken a rule. The moment plays out like a slow-motion "Oh, no!". You get that sinking feeling because you know what's coming. You realize it's just a matter of time before you get what's coming to you. There's no way you're going to get away with it. I don't think I ever cursed or said, "Shit!" or "OMG!" Those words would have meant an automatic butt whippin'.

One of the cool things we did in the country was go for walks. We had lots of room to explore to our heart's content. Sometimes (if someone had a car) we'd visit a neighbor. Maybe we'd take them some fruit, a pie, or bread. We would drop by just to say hi, see how they were doing, and catch up on the latest news. Sometimes they'd offer us tea, lemonade, or some fresh cookies they'd just baked. The kids would run around the yard playing while the grownups talked. It was a nice getaway that didn't happen often. Most of the neighbors were miles away. They were farmers too, so they were just about always working.

When we drove down the country roads (dirt and gravel mostly), we'd wave at people as we passed them and they'd wave back. Sometimes they'd stop and say hi for a few minutes, blocking the road from both directions. Taking up both sides of the road wasn't a big deal. Another car or truck might not come down the road for another half hour or more. I watched the men and how they said, "howdy".

They would bob their head up and down once, then use their index finger to acknowledge the other man . . . at least that's how my grandpa did it.

I really loved the country and spent a lot of time there. Most of it was in the summer and during school breaks. Grandpa had made a couple of tree swings from rope and carved boards for the seats. Time would fly when I was swinging. Sometimes grandma would turn on the radio and I'd sing along. I remember singing *Ring of Fire* by Johnny Cash and June Carter. (I'm not sure why it's that song that sticks out in my memory.)

Those were such good times . . . climbing trees, riding the horse, taking care of baby chicks and other animals. I have a lot of splendid memories of what it's like being a country girl. I wouldn't trade those memories for anything in the world!

My feeling like a country girl at heart, but also a city girl, was part of the deepening identity crisis I had been experiencing. I wanted to figure out my place in the world and stop feeling like an anomaly. As I entered my teenage years, my grandma and grandpa couldn't keep up the farm. My grandma got sick with cancer and stayed with us for a while. I was going through puberty and didn't understand what was going on. I remember how my grandma smelled after her chemo treatments.

When I was seventeen, my grandpa passed away in another state. Grandma was in a nursing home when he died.

Her cancer had come back and there wasn't much they could do for her. I remember visiting her in the hospital shortly before she was placed in that nursing home. She didn't even look like my grandma anymore. She had so many IVs in her and bruises from needle sticks. I remember how hard I cried. I loved my grandma, but wished she didn't have to suffer anymore. We didn't tell her about grandpa dying because she was so frail . . . but she knew.

My wish for her suffering to end came true. About two months after grandpa passed, she joined him in heaven. It completely devastated me. And just like that (finger snap), the country girl side of my life disappeared forever.

I've traveled back to their place a few times over the years, but it was different. Someone had cut down all the trees, including the fruit trees. All the out-buildings were in ruins. The three-room log cabin where I'd spent a lot of my childhood was a pile of rubble. The beautiful and green had become sick and barren, much like the landscape of my heart.

The last time I went back to their farm, there were no crops. The entire area had transformed into a meadow with wildflowers as far as the eye could see. It was beautiful. I dropped to the ground and cried my heart out. They were angry, frustrated tears. I shouted at the heavens, asking "why?". I didn't understand why things had to be the way they were! Who knows how long I sat there and cried? I just cried until I was dry.

I've not been back to my second childhood home. Maybe I will one day. That's all I have to say about that.

What Being Street Smart Taught Me

1. Learn real quick where you can and can't go.
2. Always be aware of your surroundings. You may need an escape route or makeshift weapon.
3. Friends that have your back are priceless.
4. Don't assume the cops will show up quick (or at all).
5. If a bunch of people run past you, you best start running too!
6. Snitches get stitches.
7. Walk and talk with confidence so you don't come across as weak.
8. Mind your business and stay in your own lane.

What Being Country Wise Taught Me

1. Take responsibility for your words and actions.
2. The world doesn't owe you a living . . . you owe it to yourself.
3. Learn to be self-sufficient.
4. Take care of the land and animals, and they will take care of you.
5. Never get too big for your britches.
6. You're never too old to have fun and enjoy yourself!
7. The fresh air and sunshine are healers. Make sure you get enough of both.
8. Honor is hard-won but easy to lose.

9. Sometimes the simple things are the most profound.
10. Never forget where you came from, even if it doesn't last a lifetime.

Look not at what one has, but at what they give.

Material wealth is easy to give.
How much do they give of themselves?

The true person can be easily seen by the deeds they do.
Look not upon their appearance, but into their heart.

6
War and Peace

I had to experience adult life before I could discover my place in the world. Creating my life was based on what I knew and believed. Discovering a life free from my childhood trauma would become a quest. The last two years of high school were a roller coaster ride. My senior year would be best described as a series of precipices from which I fell off. My living situation was a struggle, complete with homelessness, emotional abuse, and witnessing severe physical abuse. I often pondered whether I would make it to graduation. I had my doubts.

At times, I would get a glimpse into a possible future life. In this vision, I had a husband who didn't treat me well, two or three kids, dirt poor, and weighed somewhere around 250 pounds. This was the state of my mind back then. This scene scared the hell out of me FOR REAL. It was more frightening than snakes, the boogeyman, and all the scary movies I'd ever seen put together (except for The Exorcist).

One day, somewhere around graduation, I decided I had to get out of Arkansas. I believed that if I didn't leave my home state, the awful vision would come true. I was short on marketable skills and work experience. The only jobs I'd ever had were at fast food and pizza places. I decided I'd join the military to get out of Arkansas. The Army didn't want me. I couldn't imagine wearing those Navy uniforms, and I doubted my ability to complete Marine Corps boot camp. So, I joined the Air Force.

"Honestly, for the longest time, I was afraid to have kids."

The farthest I'd ever traveled was Georgia (the state, not the country) and Alabama (for family reunions or funerals). My first stop in becoming a member of the military was in our neighboring state of Texas. It was my first step in traveling as far away from Arkansas as possible! We should really be careful what we wish for. I got my wish to travel far away from Arkansas (my first assignment was to Japan)! When I found out where I was being sent, I cried. Fear and uncertainty washed over me (so much for the brave me). So, I did what all good active duty military members do. I followed orders and got on that plane bound for Japan! Although I didn't realize it then, God had answered my prayers.

He gave me a way out of the place where my childhood train wreck had occurred. An opportunity to explore beyond the confines of my little world.

How did I manage such a huge endeavor? I listened, followed directions, and did what I had to do (even when it was so far outside my comfort zone, I thought my body would literally explode). At some point (when we do what we think we can't), it strengthens us and makes us better equipped to handle life. I don't remember the exact date when the future vision of me being overweight with kids and an abusive husband went away, but it did. I've never seen that future vision of me again.

Lots of stuff happened over the next eleven years, four months, and twenty-five days (a military expression). I married young and my husband turned out to be just like my father. (Who would have guessed it?) Divorce would come within three years. After healing for a few years, I gave marriage a second chance. Hindsight tells me I married the opposite of my first husband, hoping for a different result. That relationship didn't work out either, and I divorced again. Within this time frame came various female problems, an early miscarriage, and a tubal pregnancy. I thought my woman parts were defective somehow. After two marriages, half of my reproductive organs were still working. I still believed (perhaps naively) I would marry again and be young enough to have children.

Honestly, for the longest time, I was afraid to have kids. Afraid I wouldn't be a wonderful mom. Afraid I might abuse my children as I had experienced growing up. Maybe that's why my pregnancies didn't work out. Once I left the military, I found another man worthy of my love. I was ready to have children, but another miscarriage and tubal pregnancy left me unable to have children. I didn't like the word sterile much. When my doctor told me the emergency surgery would leave me unable to have children, I remember his eyes welling up. It took a while to adjust to this new reality. I also figured I could adopt a child if I ever married again.

"Police with K-9 bomb dogs were everywhere."

The tensions around the world remained calm for a while. I traveled to a lot of places and learned about many cultures and languages. In Japan, I realized the older Japanese people didn't like Americans. Some Germans that didn't like Americans, but most were friendly and happy to interact. There were pro-communist areas of Italy where the people didn't believe in democracy. I understood why these Italians felt the way they did about America. Being blamed and disliked for something I had nothing to do with again reminded me of my childhood. Anyway, during this time there wasn't anything going on that required me to use my full military training.

It was the winter of 1989 when the German people grabbed their hammers, pickaxes (and any other tools they could find), and began dismantling a great wall. *The Berlin Wall* had divided their country for over twenty-eight years. I was in Sicily when "The Wall" fell. People from all over the world felt great hope for peace at that moment. After so long, the German people tasted peace and freedom! The entire world stopped to rejoice and celebrate with them!

I traveled to Berlin after this historic event in 1990. Official travel documents (in Russian) were still required to make the journey. Travelers (by car) had to pass through several checkpoints along the way. Each checkpoint included a guard building, a steel barricade across the road, and armed soldiers. A vehicle arrived at a checkpoint and a male driver would exit the car. The driver would salute the soldier, then hand over official travel papers and identification for everyone in the car. Occupants in the car sat still, looked straight ahead, and didn't make any sudden movements. The soldiers may search the car or ask other occupants to exit the vehicle to search or question them.

If everything seemed in order, the soldier would return the official papers and IDs to the male driver. The male driver would salute the soldier again, then allowed to return to their vehicle. This process would repeat itself at each checkpoint along the route into Berlin. (These were military protocols, not civilian.)

Each checkpoint had to be reached within a certain amount of time. If travelers were overdue at a checkpoint, they dispatched members of the Russian Army to locate them. Being late to your next checkpoint was to be avoided. You really didn't want the Russian military out looking for you!

I've heard many people refer to "Show me your papers." (regarding practices employed in Nazi Germany) over the last few years. The reason they refer to this act so often is that it's not something people want, regardless of whether they realize it. Lots of things could go sideways quick at a checkpoint. If your papers or identification aren't in order, or they find anything suspicious, stuff could go sideways real quick. If they find banned items in your car, or you break some new rule that popped up overnight, things could get ugly. Trust me, I lived it.

After arriving in West Berlin, things were not so tense. The locals were celebrating The Wall coming down. The reunification of their country was on the horizon. Optimism and hope were thick in the air. You could feel it in your bones. While in West Berlin, I stepped through a hole in The Wall into the former East Berlin. Someone had chiseled a hole (barely large enough for a person to fit in sideways) in the concrete. The spot where I stood had been in the "kill zone" less than six months before.

What that means is, if I had stood on that exact spot before November 1989, guards in the watchtower would
have shot me dead. It was one of the eeriest feelings I
have ever experienced.

The Berlin Wall coming down was a magical time in
history! It was hope realized after years of oppression.
The hope all people would know peace (after so many
years of war and strife). When I hear the haunting whistle
of Klaus Meine (lead singer of The Scorpions), it gives me
goose bumps to this day. As I listen to the lyrics, "Take
me to the magic of the moment on a glory night, where
the children of tomorrow dream away in the wind of
change.", chills run down my spine. This special song,
aptly named *Wind of Change*, will always be my reminder
of that glorious moment when The Wall fell and hope re-
newed for the world.

In 1991, I traveled from Germany to Ohio for training.
The peace the world had experienced since the fall of The
Wall only lasted eight months. Tensions had been rising
around the world since the previous August. Diplomatic
meetings failed, and they could not agree on terms to re-
solve the conflict. One morning, on my way to class, I
spotted a newspaper with the headline, "US at War!" One
Persian Gulf nation had invaded another and thus began
yet another war.

It was one of those pivotal moments in my life. I asked
myself tough questions and answered them honestly. The
last thing I wanted was another war and more killing.

I had been around *The Holy Bible* my entire childhood. One of The Ten Commandments states, "Thou shall not kill." I hoped they wouldn't send us to war. Honestly, I didn't want anyone to go to war (us or them). But I also knew if I were called, I would go. I would do my duty and uphold the oath I had taken. I had no choice (other than an extended visit to Leavenworth). Realizing this possibility made me sad beyond words, and it created a knot in the pit of my stomach. Even so, I woke up the next day, put on my "serious Sergeant" face, and went to class.

A few days later, I was on a plane headed back to Germany. In the short time I'd been away, everything had changed. Security was tight, and tension was thick in the air. Police with K-9 bomb dogs were everywhere. It seems like we stayed on high threat alert for months. Service members get used to the possibility of being shot or blown up at any moment. It really helps put your life (and choices) in perspective.

I spent most of my day checking for traps on doors, using mirrors to spot explosive devices, and looking for trip wires. I was looking for anything out of place. Getting blown up in your car is a bad way to start the day. Not showing your ID or access card fast enough (or stepping over some imaginary line nobody told you about) and getting jacked up by military police isn't much fun either.

We all practiced our security guard skills. I'm not talking security like you might see at a mall or an office building.

I'm talking about protecting important places (like utilities, weapons, and drinking water). We were well-armed and ready for anything. If you (or anyone else) don't do their best at security, you (or your teammates) could get shot, blown to bits, or exposed to some nasty chemical. Either way, people die and their next of kin gets a knock on their door.

Another fun part of living under high threat alert was strapping on a gas mask, utility belt, helmet, and chemical gear, then trying to use the bathroom. This task was easier for guys (obviously). Carrying all your gear on you (plus your weapons and pack) while being outside on a seventy plus degrees (Fahrenheit) day or a single digit degrees night was challenging. Either scenario could easily bring about a medical emergency if you weren't prepared and hydrated. No one wants to be called a dumbass for experiencing hypothermia or heat stroke.

"I saw myself high atop the world's largest roller coaster, about to drop straight down . . ."

Oh yeah, and you better hope when shit hits the fan, and the alarm sounds you're not in the john in the middle of something. You have about twenty-seconds to seal yourself up (in your chemical gear) or face the possibility of chemical exposure and a slow, very painful death. Not fun!

If you do get exposed to some manmade hell, you pray it kills you quick. You pray it's not something that rots you slowly from the inside or peels your skin off like a bell pepper on a barbecue grill. You don't want to choke on your own lungs, finding it harder and harder to breathe until you can't get any air, pass out, and your heart stops. No, you want it over quick. You don't want to know what hit you. There's nothing worse than dying a slow death, realizing you're dying, and knowing there's not a damn thing you can do about it. (Okay, maybe being burned alive would be worse.)

All these events and situations made me realize I was no longer suited for the military. It wasn't just the war and other world tensions. I started feeling like I didn't belong. The military was changing, and I didn't like the changes. I had two years left on my contract, so I did the best I could, having lost faith in the only job I'd ever known. My physical condition was poor, with no solution in sight after about two years of multiple doctor visits and therapy. Military medicine was all about med's and "stop whining". Man, they loved prescribing Motrin (Ibuprofen)! It was like their magic cure (much like Robitussin or Vicks Vapor Rub was to our mom when we were children). They weren't huge about rehab (at least not for long). If a soldier didn't meet fitness standards, or couldn't deploy, they usually booted them out (discharged them).

I lost my worldwide deployable status after my last visit to a specialist. I was about to face a medical retirement or discharge.

Maybe it was me who was changing. I'd learned a lot, visited many places, and was a stronger woman and adult. My view of the world had changed. I now saw it as one big place where most people just want to live a safe and happy life. A place where powerful people (or downright evil ones) make decisions that negatively affect other people and cause suffering. A world where there are people so far out on the edge they do unspeakable things. Suffering is caused by the actions (or inaction) of people.

The similarities between people of different countries and beliefs started registering in my conscious mind. My intuitive ability to know things would gently return, helping me see a more global perspective. This Buddha instinct would give me moments of clarity. I believe that people all over the world want the same things I do (mostly). I realized we all want to be loved, have shelter, friends, family, safety, feel useful and needed, find our place in the world, and experience happiness. These were my observations.These topics aren't what most military people talk about (at least not in groups or mixed company).

The universe heard my prayer to end my military career. Congress mandated a reduction in force of the active-duty military.

My branch of service offered a deal to certain members within designated specialty codes (our specific job). If they volunteered to get out, they could receive tens of thousands of dollars (based on their rank and time in service). If the service didn't get the numbers of volunteers they needed, they would involuntarily separate members until they reached their quota. Those forced out would only receive a few thousand dollars. (Military members had to fulfill their contract for the full term. If they didn't, they could face a Courts-Martial or a bad discharge. That same contract was at the convenience of the government. At that moment, it wasn't convenient anymore.) It took me about a whole thirty-seconds to decide to take the deal. I felt it was time to go.

Even though I was afraid and second-guessed my choice to leave the military, something compelled me to go. Making my next rank (promotion) was the only thing that could save me from being discharged. I looked at it as a sign from God. If I made my promotion, the universe was telling me to stay. If I didn't get promoted, it was affirming it was time to say goodbye to what had been my whole adult life up to that point.

The promotion results came out a few weeks before my projected discharge date. I didn't make the cut-off for promotion to the next rank. I recall missing it by less than two points or something crazy like that. Although it bummed me out, I felt the universe had spoken. The promotion score was a two-fold message.

I was smart enough to succeed and only had to figure out what I wanted to succeed at. Once I accepted the fact I was leaving the military, I was still scared, but it was an exciting scary. It had the attitude of going on a new adventure. I saw myself high atop the world's largest roller coaster, about to drop straight down at an incredible speed. All I could think of or say was, "Bring it!"

In the military, I took an oath to defend my country against all enemies . . . foreign and domestic. I kept my oath over all the years I served. I still hold that oath as a sacred trust. As I look back on all of this now, I can honestly say joining the military was one of the best decisions I ever made in my life.

Once I was out of the military, I moved to a state that I'd never lived in nor visited for more than a couple of days. My job search took a while. There weren't a lot of jobs, but I don't think I knew how to look for a job. I had no clue what kind of job I could do in the civilian world. The military had been my job for over eleven years. There weren't tons of companies looking for chemical warfare or communication specialists. My computer and network administration skills were valuable, but I didn't have a degree. My skills (and responsibilities) were usually greater than other people my age. I landed lots of interviews, but only secured a part-time seasonal job at a tax preparation business. One (of the many) job interviews stands out in my mind.

The interviewer asked me what level of responsibility I'd had in a previous position. When I told him, he didn't believe me! He basically called me a liar without having the intestinal fortitude to call it as he saw it. It devastated me. After all my military training and experience (and honorable service to my country), I was being called a liar. Even though I badly needed a job at that point, I could not allow my honor to be questioned. Using a calm voice, I told the employer I was not a liar. I also informed him he didn't have a clue what the military was about, the level of responsibility of its members, or anything about me. I told him he had insulted my integrity and that the interview was over.

Yep, I ended the interview, stood up with my head held high, and walked out. I had never done that before . . . or since. I have wondered how the employer felt about being called out on his bullshit. Was it the only time someone shut him down and stopped his bullying? Maybe he thought twice about how to treat veterans (and women) in the future. It's my hope he learned something. I know I did.

After I left the military, I tried enrolling in college and securing a job. My need to find my place in the world kept growing. After I found a part-time job and enrolled in two college classes, I still wasn't happy. Finances, school, and life was a struggle. My new life moved much slower than my military life had (okay, it was boring me to death).

A change was needed (or I'd go crazy), but I didn't know what the change was. I asked for help and in short order; the universe answered my prayers with a big slap upside the head I never saw coming.

What Being in the Military Taught Me

1. Don't be so quick to jump to conclusions. Take a step back, see the big picture, THEN act.
2. The greatest gift is people who have your six (and you theirs).
3. Military members didn't see color when I was serving. They saw team members (for any of which they would give their life).
4. The eyes can deceive. Trust your instincts.
5. Do more and talk less. You learn more by watching, doing, and asking questions.
6. When shit hits the fan, your greatest weapon is your brain. Stay calm and remember your training.
7. Stay proficient with your weapons and equipment. They are an extension of you.
8. Always have a plan A . . . and B . . . and C.
9. Enrich your life by experiencing different languages, countries, and cultures.
10. Do not tell anyone about what you have or where it's located.

Driving home from class this evening, the sun was finishing its set.
The peaks were shrouded in rain clouds of gray.
A rainbow stood on end atop one of those last-minute, illuminated peaks.

I thought to myself, "How would I answer if asked where heaven was at that moment?"
I would point to that peak and say, "Heaven is right there where the rainbow stands in light and clouds.

That is heaven . . . where it is . . . what it looks like."

The rainbow only lasted a short time and then was gone.
The light did fade from Grandmother's great face.

To me, here on this earth and in this life, we only get to see heaven every now and then . . .
in bits and pieces . . .
if we take the time to look around.

I think today was a bits and pieces day.
And my heart was glad from it.

7
Crazy White Girl
Mental Breakdown

Yep, I think most times we should really be careful what we wish for. I believe our prayers are always answered in a way that's best for us, even if it's difficult or uncomfortable. My slap upside the head was exactly what I needed to pull my head out of my butt (where it had been for far too long). (Much later, I learned I could ask for my prayers to be answered gently, but gentle wasn't really what I needed back then.) My wake-up call came as a release of twenty years of crap and illusion. This single-day completely changed the course of my life and allowed the white woman to become the Indian she'd always believed herself to be.

It was a warm spring day less than a year after my military career had ended. I was trying to start a new life in a state I'd never lived. Finding a job proved difficult, but I found a part-time position. The financial support I'd counted on to pay my school tuition was delayed.

My college classes were boring, and I didn't really like the area where I had moved. I guess you could say I didn't belong there, or it wasn't the place for me.

"The feeling of my body literally exploding and my body bits coating the backyard like some macabre murder scene . . ."

The day my life fell apart seems like yesterday. I woke up feeling anxious and out of sorts. My daily routine had become simply going through the motions of life. I was restless and felt the need to get away and go somewhere . . . ANYWHERE! Walking seemed to be a good choice to help release some of my built-up energy. Sometimes I walked as fast as I could and other times I ran. The feeling of running from something . . . running to something . . . filled my entire being. I didn't understand what was going on. It was like I was not the one in control anymore.

It was late afternoon when I realized I had walked quite a distance from my house. An urgent need to get back home (before it was too dark to see) came into my awareness. An emotion started building in me then that I couldn't quite describe. The closer I got to home, the bigger it became. I'd never felt this kind of emotion before, and it scared me. For a moment, I thought I might go crazy.

Looking up, I noticed the sky turning dark. A big storm was moving in. The air turned humid, the pressure rose, and the wind picked up. This, too, seemed to increase the bigness of the feeling inside me. I walked faster. My legs were tired and shook, but I kept walking as fast as I could. I couldn't stop . . . didn't want to stop. Right then, I thought I would be perfectly okay with losing consciousness and dying right there. My mind was beyond caring. Then I realized this was the answer I'd been searching for to explain why I'd been feeling the empty "nothingness" and just going through the motions of life. I didn't care if I lived or died! Nothing was working . . . nothing gave me joy . . . I had no purpose. I was like a feather in the wind, floating aimlessly through life.

I finally made it safely back to my house. Now the winds were howling and a pouring rain came. Lightning lit up the sky and was so loud it could scare the bejeezus out of the strongest person. All the hours I'd spent trying to walk off the weird energy hadn't worked. The huge nothingness and unnamed feeling were still inside me. I couldn't stay inside! Something prompted me to go outside. I had to go outside!

I wasn't afraid to go out into the storm. Maybe subconsciously I remembered the young girl who loved sitting outside during thunderstorms. She would listen to the thunder clapping and watch the lightning flash in the sky. She felt a power in them that was hard to explain.

My smaller version got into trouble more than once for not coming in out of a storm.

I opened the door and stepped out into the backyard. The strong wind pushed the heavy rain sideways, stinging my face and arms. Lightning was lighting up the now dark sky like those photos of desert thunderstorms out west. It seems I stood there for a few minutes, not knowing what to do. I felt how I imagined a caged animal would feel. That weird energy inside me was so big that I felt I would explode!

I'm not sure if a human can spontaneously combust or implode, but that's what I thought might happen at that moment. I felt like I was having a "crazy, white girl, mental breakdown". The feeling of my body literally exploding and my body bits coating the backyard like some macabre murder scene from the best horror flick of all time crossed my mind. I wasn't sure what was about to happen, but happen it did.

I suddenly let out the longest, loudest, ear-piercing scream I think I've ever released in my life. A scream that came from somewhere deep inside my soul. Such a scream is so spine-tingling it scares the crap out of you and anyone else within earshot! Fortunately, the storm was louder than my soul-wrenching scream that night. I can only imagine the ensuing pandemonium had my neighbors heard my scream, called 9-1-1, and swore a person next door was being murdered!

At some point, I sat down on the rain-soaked grass and cried. I cried out loud. I seem to remember cursing and arguing at something . . . someone . . . maybe God. I cried and cried. I'm talking body-shaking sobs I had no control over. My crying went on for what seemed like hours. I don't remember hearing the thunder, seeing the lightning, or feeling the rain at all once I loosed the scream. I cried until I couldn't cry anymore.

"We don't know we are living a lie."

When I felt the first few moments of internal peace, I realized what had happened and why it had happened. My whole life I did what I was supposed to do, tried to please people, be the peacemaker, and thinking I could control things out of my control. That day I knew deep down in my soul my life wasn't working. My life hadn't worked for quite some time. It had all been a lie, and I realized I couldn't live the lie anymore.

Back inside the house, I was at peace because I had realized the truth. I remember sleeping the "sleep of the dead" that night. All the walking and releasing of tears had drained every ounce of my energy. Years of misconception, training, false beliefs, frustration, fear, grief, shame, and guilt had released. It was the starting point for the next phase of my life.

Doing all the things I was supposed to do . . . taught to do . . . hadn't worked.

I was lost in a world I had never known as an adult. I started thinking about what was missing. What was the answer to being happy and feeling like I belonged? I had tried the traditional teachings and lessons and they hadn't worked. I thought about my Irish, Scottish, and Native American ancestry. Maybe one of them had a better way of living. A way that would help me find my place, purpose, and inner peace.

My mind raced back to childhood and my days of playing Indian. Even after twenty-something years, I still felt kinship with Native Americans. I decided at that moment to learn all I could about American Indian history and culture. Finally, I had hope and direction. Perhaps the Indian way of life would be better than the one I'd lived for thirty years. Better than thirty years of fairy tales, illusions, and believable lies.

I went to a bookstore and *Spirit Song* by Mary Summer Rain jumped out at me. I bought it and read it like a sponge soaking up water. Some passages resonated with me so much! A sense of peace came over me while reading that book. I later found a suggested reading list of Native American history books. I began reading each one until I had basically read them all. Some books dated back to the 1800s, and were as old as I remember my grandpa being when I was a child.

The books I read made me laugh, cry, feel empty, feel ashamed, and also feel pure anger.

Some of the most profound were *Bury My Heart at Wounded Knee* by Dee Brown; *God is Red* by Vine Deloria, Jr., *Black Elk Speaks* by John G. Neihardt; and *In the Spirit of Crazy Horse* by Peter Matthiesson. From these books, I learned that the history they taught us in school was one-sided and not the whole truth. Some of what I learned made me angry because I felt lied to about so many things! I realized the reason I felt so empty and confused was that I had been living a lie my whole life!

It was like all the lies (illusions) smacked me upside the head one day. At that moment, I clearly saw the lie I had been living all along. At first, I thought I had wasted a sizeable part of my life. Later, I realized I had woken up to the lie when I was ready to wake up. I woke up when it was MY time to wake up.

We don't know we are living a lie. We are just mimicking our teachings and what we ended up believing through our experiences. It's like believing in Santa Claus as a kid, then one day (when you're older) you find out the truth about jolly ole St. Nick. You feel betrayed . . . tricked . . . manipulated. Know what I mean? Once you discover one truth, your mind asks other questions. Questions like "What other lies have I been told and accepted as true?".

For years, I read anything I could get my hands on related to Native American history. I had two library cards and was checking out all the American Indian books they had.

Discovering Native American flute and pow-wow music expanded my appreciation for their culture. One eye-opening lesson was the conquerors write history, and the defeated seldom get to tell their side of the story. Millions of indigenous peoples of the Americas vanished from hunger, disease, slavery, murder, war, and forced marches. All this knowledge made my heart was sad, but it also found its home.

"Perhaps they would have seen a dirty, extra-pale, white woman who was probably on crack or meth."

I became friends with a Native American elder (Silver Eagle) who gave me advice and encouragement. I was hesitant because of my extra white skin and blue eyes. My elder friend told me I only needed one drop of native blood. I also came to believe that if the heart is red (having a kinship with Native America), one doesn't need that drop. There are Rainbow People (people with red hearts and many skin colors) out in the world. They support native peoples and keep native traditions alive in their own way (without dishonoring them). The more I learned about the different cultures of the Native American nations, the more I wanted to know my purpose. I had lost it somewhere along my life travels. While in the military, I knew my mission and purpose.

After returning to "the real world", I hadn't yet found it. I guess I was a wandering, lost soul at that point.

I decided I would do a Vision Quest to find peace and discover my part in the world. My friend Silver Eagle guided me on how to prepare for my quest, but my fear of going out in the woods alone for four days was a genuine concern. Having a man I could trust to watch over me for those four days was crucial. Finding the perfect spot within the vast wilderness of Utah was very important. It seemed like a daunting task, so I waited and prayed for everything to fall into place.

Before long, the universe sent me my hunka kola (best friend, like a brother from another mother). John owned land on top of a mountain. I could talk to him about what I'd learned and adopted into my life. He was a country boy (raised Mormon), but listened with an open mind. We had in common being military veterans. I looked past him being a squid, and he forgave me for being "chair force" (military humor). He graciously agreed to help me with my first Vision Quest.

With the help of my elder friend Silver Eagle, I prepared for my quest over many days. I ate less and less food each day until I was fasting and my stomach stopped rebelling. Listening to my elder's advice, I prayed while preparing myself and creating my offerings for the journey. I even took some herbs to make sure I wouldn't start my cycle during my four-day quest.

The quest day came, and we trekked up the mountain by truck and on foot. After we arrived on "Big M", I spent some time selecting my spot. I made the spot sacred for what I was doing and asking for. The prayers were said, the circle created, and the offerings given. I also made a bed of sage leaves where I could sit or lie down during my quest.

I spent four days on that mountain. The scorching sun beat down on me by day and the chilly nights left me shivering. Sleep was minimal, more like a series of disoriented naps. I had nothing to eat or drink, moistened my lips from a naturally carved rock birdbath, and wore nothing but a buckskin bikini. I prayed, sang, cried, and dreamed.

I'm sure if anyone had seen me, they would have thought I had lost my mind. Perhaps they would have seen a dirty, extra-pale, white woman who was probably on crack or meth. I looked a big 'ol mess, but I was happy because I had found my place and purpose during those four days! The commitment I made up on that mountain was to walk The Red Road (live a good and honorable life). It was the greatest gift anyone could have given me. I made the choice to live as close to the native way as possible, and never went back to the "civilized" version of living.

For my second Vision Quest, I gradually reduced my food intake as I had before my first quest. Traveling to my spot high in the Wasatch Range took most of the day.

I hadn't been this high in elevation (about nine thousand feet) during my first vision quest. When I arrived, the temperature was around seventy-degrees Fahrenheit (in the sun) with a chilly breeze whipping around.

"Suddenly my brain was fully awake and my mind was screaming . . . SNAKE!"

This time, I had a makeshift shelter and didn't have to spend my days outside. I did the normal things like creating my sacred space, praying with my pipe, and singing. As the sun set on my first day, the temperature dropped. The wind picked up and my shelter didn't have heat. The chilly wind and frosty temperatures laughed at all my layers of clothing. It became so cold that my teeth started chattering, making what sounded like the noise from the spinning rotor blades of a helicopter. It was cold enough if you didn't warm yourself up within a few minutes, the shivering would stop, you would feel warm again, then go to sleep forever.

Crawling into my negative twenty-degree rated sleeping bag, it only took a few minutes before I was warm again. I tried to stay awake, pray, and sing, but the warmth and cozy knocked me out. The next thing I knew, I was half awake and felt something . . . something on my leg . . . I thought I was dreaming . . . then I felt it again!

A hazy thought drifted into my sleepy mind . . . "You're in a makeshift shelter, up on a mountain, and there's something in your bag with you." Suddenly, my brain was fully awake and my mind was screaming . . . SNAKE! Holy shit!

I tried to claw my way out of the top of the sleeping bag, but I couldn't push myself out! I desperately pulled on the inside zipper. Whatever had joined me in my bag was now moving around like crazy, too! Oh my God! I was screaming and fighting my way out of that sleeping bag with everything I had!

I finally unzipped the bag far enough to get free, jump up, and run to the edge of my shelter. As I turned to look back toward my now vacated sleeping bag, my visitor came screaming out of it! I was screaming . . . it was screaming! Through my terror (and all the screaming), my brain said, "Snakes don't scream." I looked again and saw a striped tail and brown fur. It was a chipmunk! It had run to the opposite corner of my shelter, screaming and breathing really fast, just like me! Still breathing heavily, our hearts racing, we both got real still and quiet and stared at each other.

My brain needed about fifteen-seconds to register what had just happened. Suddenly, I started laughing hysterically! I'm talking the uncontrollable, eyes watering and stomach hurting kind of laugh.

I wondered if the chipmunk realized how funny the whole thing was as well. Apparently, he was cold and just wanted a warm place to snuggle like me!

We made friends, and I apologized for scaring him almost to death. I told him he could come back anytime he got cold, but to please give me some advanced warning next time! Now, every time I see a chipmunk, I laugh and remember that frosty night high in the Wasatch Mountains.

"... life would gift me with a deeper understanding of the word bizarre."

Releasing all those emotions, playing Indian for so long, and studying American Indian history and culture also helped me understand Indian humor. The not-so-good part about getting native humor is being so white it makes you stand out like a sore thumb. My "stand out" for this new revelation happened in a movie theater.

The movie adaptation of the Sherman Alexie novel *The Lone Ranger and Tonto Fistfight in Heaven* came out in theaters. I was so excited to go! It was a brilliant book, and I thought it would be a good movie. The twist to this story was playing in the background while I remained unaware of its comedic irony.

At that time, I was living right smack dab in the middle of Zion (according to The Church of Jesus Christ of Latter-Day Saints-LDS).

I had given no thought to this mixture of my skin tone, my background, LDS country, and an Indian movie. Arriving at the theater, I hurriedly got my ticket and headed in to watch *Smoke Signals*.

Most of the audience shared my skin tone. I took notice but was used to it (having gotten over the initial culture shock since moving there a few years before). Now I really didn't expect a busload of real Indians fresh off the Rez (reservation) to show up (although it would have made the experience less awkward for me). I expected the usual laughter at funny moments and tears at the sad ones, like at most movie showings. The movie goers were invested in the characters, followed the plot twists, felt the sad moments, but didn't get the humor. Let me try to explain . . .

There's a scene where the main characters hitch a ride off the Rez from one of their friends that has a car that actually runs. Once they get in the back seat, they duck down. Their friend starts her car, turns around (looking out the rear windshield), and drives the entire way off the Rez in reverse! I cracked up laughing because either she was Heyoka (a person who does things opposite of the way everyone else does them) or the car could only be driven in reverse! Both scenarios were funny as heck! Then I realized there were only two or three other people in the whole movie theater laughing.

I immediately got the feeling everyone was staring at me, wondering, "What the heck's so funny, white girl?"

Maybe everyone wasn't staring at me, but it sure seemed like they were. I felt uncomfortable being white on the outside and red on the inside. Perhaps that's why I felt the way I did when my laugh stuck out in the theater. Who can say for sure? I know that Indian humor works like any other humor. It's tied to the culture and experiences of the people. You either get it or you don't. What I learned that day was to keep my reactions silent in a mixed crowd because you never know how others may react.

I wondered who the other people were that laughed at that scene with me. I think maybe we could have been good friends and shared our own Indian humor for years to come. In reality, movies end, people go home, and they never know the people they shared a movie laugh with. Life is just bizarre like that.

In the years following my Indian movie experience, life would gift me with a deeper understanding of the word bizarre. It would also familiarize me with many other adjectives I would have rather not known.

What My Mental Breakdown Taught Me

1. Don't hold in all the negative stuff from your life.
2. Release any negative you've been carrying around. If you don't release it, it will find a way out on its own.
3. If the way you've been living your life isn't working . . . do something different!

4. Never stop learning. Pick up a book or take a class so your brain won't shrivel up and die.

5. Don't sleepwalk through life! Pay attention and you will wake up to the lies that have kept you imprisoned.

6. Find what stirs your passion and creativity, then do those things! Live your life!

7. You are stronger than you ever believed possible! Stop making excuses and take action to make life better.

8. Sometimes our fears are far greater than anything that befalls us.

9. Critters need warm snuggles! Humans scare the crap out of them too!

10. Life is much better if you have a sense of humor. Laugh often!

11. You can't live your life being two different people. Be the one you truly are!

12. Every experience we have contains a lesson. Be open to the lesson.

13. History isn't an accurate recounting of events. It has a "spin" based on who did the recounting. Much like the "news" media of today tells you what they want you to hear, not necessarily the truth.

Do not forever live in the past, nor see anything but the future.
For one day you may wake and find . . . life has passed you by.

8
A Forgotten Father

Sometimes I think it's a good thing to only have one major life trauma going on at a time. During the late nineties, I had two going on, but divine intervention ensured I only knew about one. Had I known about the second while the first was going on, I might have lost my mind. I have heard many times, "God won't put more on you than you can handle." My take on that saying is a little different, but I think that's exactly what happened in this case. It's not a good idea to open more than one skeleton closet at a time. So, one remained closed until opening it was right for me. The door to that closet had my dad's name written on it.

My formative years were chock full of fear and not knowing what might come next. My father was an alcoholic and what many would label a mean drunk. He was a decent man when he was sober, trouble was he was never sober for long. We never knew what mood he would be in or what might set him off.

It took little for him to get into a heated argument with my mom or fly into a rage over practically anything. Once my dad lost his hair-trigger temper, he became violent. His preferred methods of mayhem were throwing things, physical assault, and whippings with a belt. He would beat up my mom, punch my older brother, and frequently apply his belt without mercy.

The things going on inside our home were actually worse than the endless bullying, fights, and ongoing racial tensions happening outside our home. At least I kind of knew what to expect once I stepped outside our door. A normal day at home might include physical abuse, screaming, berating, items thrown at us, cursing, holes punched in the wall, and the sound of things breaking. A quiet day without some type of violence seemed rare. Sometimes when stuff was terrible, I'd hide way up in the tree in our backyard.

"My life was already past a seven-layer dip of insanity . . ."

I'm not writing this story looking for pity because my life was fair to partly crappy growing up. It's just what it was. My mom and dad had a drama-filled relationship, mostly because of his alcohol addiction. As kids, my siblings and I learned to play games like "walk on eggshells"; "make yourself invisible"; and "hide on top of the shed".

These games were not fun ones kids like to play, but ones we played to stay out of trouble. This crazy life of drunk and disorderly, domestic violence, disturbing the peace, and trips to the state penitentiary went on for years.

One day, the cops showed up after my mom drew a pistol on my dad. The police took my dad away in handcuffs (justifiably so). My mom had finally had enough of the abuse. Shortly after that incident, we moved away from the house on Marshall Street. We didn't have to walk down that alley to school anymore. It was like an early Christmas present!

Mom worked a lot to take care of us. Understandably, she didn't want us to see our dad ever again. I understood why, but sometimes I would ask her about him and she would just say we couldn't see him. I knew why she did it. She wanted to keep us safe. But sometimes it was just weird not having a dad around. I believed everyone had fathers at home except us (this probably wasn't the case, but it sure felt like it at the time).

After a while, I stopped asking about my dad. I grew up and started my own life. Now and then I'd wonder where he was, what he was doing, and if he'd ever quit drinking. Stuff like that. I'd think about finding him, but then I'd convince myself that he probably didn't want to hear from me. I figured he had a new life, or maybe he didn't even remember his kids. It's funny the stuff that goes through your mind. I bet half of it wasn't even true.

One day (while sorting through my mom's important papers), I discovered a copy of his death certificate. He had died twelve years earlier. It was a weird and awkward moment. It's like I woke up one day and "poof!", I didn't have a dad anymore. To never see his children again must have been sad and heartbreaking for my father. This probably didn't have a positive effect on his drinking problem. His children didn't know he had died and had no time to grieve.

I couldn't go back in time and talk to him to get his perspective on things. There was no way for me to understand what went on or get closure. No way to say my last goodbye. He was still a part of me, even though I hadn't laid eyes on him for thirty years before his death. Your family is always going to be your family. I carry within me half his DNA, so there is a bond that will always exist.

At the time he died, I was a witness in a doozie of a court case, so I'm grateful I didn't find out about his death during the two trials I had to endure. My life was already past a seven-layer dip of insanity and knowing of his death would have added another layer. It seems everything played out the way it did, so I wouldn't know the exact time he died. That's a whole other perspective to come from on the "God stepped in" theory. It is like this infinite chessboard. The pieces move around without your conscious awareness, and they design the strategy for you to win every time. The result will always be what's best for you (though you may not realize it at the time).

This is all pretty cool in my book. Creator . . . the master chess player . . . the Obi-Wan of board games . . . the Gandalf of possibilities.

"I think it's important to recognize when you're healed and move on with life."

I think about two years passed before I tracked down where my dad was buried. He served in the Army during the Korean War. Not sure if he was "in country" or saw combat, but I thought maybe it was the reason he drank. Things we experience in wartime hang on like a monkey on our back. Any substance that dulls the pain, silences the dreams, or stops the flashbacks becomes our way of coping. Yeah, maybe that's what happened.

When I was a child, I thought it was me that made him drink. I believed I did and said things that pissed him off. I constantly tried to figure out what I could do to stop making him mad all the time. This made me feel like a terrible child who didn't know how to behave. After I was grown, I realized I had nothing to do with it (but the damage was done). It was the alcohol that did it. Alcohol brings out whatever you've got swirling around inside you. I guess that's how someone came up with the term mean drunk.

Last year, I went and visited his grave at our National Veterans Cemetery.

I finally did some crying and asked him some of those questions I'd been waiting to ask for decades. (It's amazing how long we carry shit around that we don't need.) After all those years, I felt his presence with me at his grave that day. He answered all the questions I'd had over the years. I received a most sincere apology from him and did a lot of healing that day.

I can't say I understand what my father went through in life, but I forgave him a long time ago. Visiting his grave gave me the closure I needed for that chapter of my life. I think God helps us heal in ways we don't realize. You don't have to believe the spirit of those who've passed can communicate to help us heal, but I think it's important to recognize when you're healed and move on with life.

Some may get the impression my dad was a real douchebag. I never judged him that way. He taught me a lot. All the stuff I experienced as a kid with my dad has helped me later in life with jobs, dealing with alcoholics and drug-addicted people, setting my boundaries, staying sober, and the list goes on and on. If I hadn't had those experiences, I wouldn't be able to relate to people with the same issues I lived through. In my profession, I've helped many people because I knew where they were coming from . . . and they knew I knew.

I believe everyone is a teacher. Some teach us stuff we should not do. We can learn precious lessons from their mistakes or choices.

Some teach us stuff we want to make sure we do, so we'll be happy and successful or whatever. Look at all the people who've come and gone in your life (from your preschool teacher or babysitter to your high school teachers and beyond). Write down everything you learned from them—good or bad. This will be an eye-opening experience (if you actually do it). A lot of things will finally make sense to you.

A few years back, my best friend asked me to tell her about one memory I had of my dad. It took me a few moments to recall one. When I did, I replied, "Throwing bricks at my dad from atop the shed in the backyard." I don't think it was anywhere near the answer she was expecting. In all honesty, it wasn't the memory I was hoping to recall, either. As I reflected on this memory, I thought it a pretty sad reflection of what my relationship had been with my dad. My mind had searched for a positive memory to share with my friend, and having found none, shared a less horrible one.

Why had I thrown bricks at my dad from atop a shed? It was preservation and resolution. He was on a drunken rampage. The roof of the shed offered safety and the advantage of stealth. If the bricks injured or knocked him out, his rampage would end. This was the logic of an abused child.

My father passed away one week before my thirty-fifth birthday. He died from lung cancer that had spread to his spinal cord.

Basically, it became harder and harder for him to breathe until his respiratory system (lungs) shut down. He was only sixty-five years old. In an odd coincidence, his last address was one block over from where my mom had moved the family after they'd split up. Life does indeed work in mysterious ways.

I think my dad died from the inside out. He had too many years of drinking alcohol and smoking. Maybe his heart was broken as well. Regardless, it seems he never let go of the past or freed himself from his demons. Disease develops in our body when we don't release past negative. It's usually some form of cancer that slowly kills various parts of the body. (This has been my experience.) Sadly, his death wouldn't be the last that ended this way.

What My Father Taught Me

1. Drinking is not a good thing. It only numbs you from your life's traumas for a while. Your "ghosts" will still be there when you sober up. Release and heal the past so you don't feel the need to drink.

2. If you have people who love you, it's a gift. Treasure it. Treat them better than you treat anyone else. Have their back and tell them you love them. Give them a hug and mean it!

3. It's not appropriate to abuse anyone in any way! Live by The Golden Rule and treat others how you want to be treated.

4. The best thing you can do for a person who's addicted to alcohol or drugs is stop enabling them and walk away. Sometimes love is walking away!

5. Don't blame yourself for the actions of others. Only you have control over yourself!

6. You cannot save anyone but yourself. Let other people save themselves.

7. Save yourself! If you're weak, you cannot be strong for yourself or others.

8. Do not fill your heart with emptiness, anger, hate, jealousy, revenge, or any other negative emotion. Fill your heart with love (even if it's just a little) and send out love instead. What you send out comes back to you!

9. A father's love is forever, even if no one realizes it until they are gone.

10. Do not hold stuff inside. Release it or it will find a way out (usually through addiction, negative behavior, disease, or psychological damage).

11. Children's psyches, behaviors, and beliefs form during their early years. Be an excellent role model for them. What you do (or do not) teach them will have a direct effect on the world, good or bad.

We cannot live our lives telling ourselves . . .
"If only . . ."

9
Sudden Death

As we grow older, it's only natural that relatives older than us will pass on. Not that it's easy or predictable, but we kind of operate from that assumption. It's much harder to understand (and come to terms with) when it's someone younger than us. Two things I've learned from my limited number of years . . .

1. We don't know how things will turn out in the future.
2. Younger family members may cross over before the older ones.

A Garth Brooks song is playing in my head as I write these words. "Now, I'm glad I didn't know the way it all would end, the way it all would go. Our lives are better left to chance. I could have missed the pain, but I'd of had to miss the dance." It's been this way for me twice. I'll tell you about the first one now.

The second, I'll leave to its place in time in this book. It's hard for me to know where to start, as there's so much to tell. I guess I'll start at the beginning and tell you how it came to be that a younger relative died before me.

"So, I stood there, frozen in place, and cried."

Is there one sibling that brothers and sisters rally behind more than the others? It's a question I've contemplated many times. My younger brother, Charlie, was that sibling. He had a lifelong medical condition that caused a myriad of difficulties for him. In his youth, there were multiple trips to the hospital via ambulance. I remember several times my mom frantically driving him to the emergency room, praying she would get him there in time. His medical condition made him different from other kids.

When he started school, the kids would ruthlessly tease and bully him. We tried our best to keep an eye on him and have his back. Someone picking on my brother made me go full-on crazy. I got into many a fight protecting him, and so did my other siblings. No matter how big the bully was (or how many there were), the fight was on! After a while, the word got out and nobody wanted "the crazy" unleashed on them, so they backed off a bit.

As my brother grew older, he didn't always make the best decisions, but he would be straight with you.

He was a kid at heart and had a sense of humor. No matter what, he loved his family. He had that gratefulness in him. Most of all, he never gave up. Even after discovering bits of his memory gone and having to re-learn (multiple times) simple tasks such as math or reading a ruler. Even when he lost a job (because of his medical condition) and spent months looking for a new one. He simply kept chugging along, doing the best he could in life.

He drove non-stop, cross-country once, just to visit his nephews for a few days. He always had the backs of his family. My nephews had great fun when they went with him to Chuckie Cheese. He loved his nephews to death, and they nicknamed him Uncle Cheese. His brothers and sisters still called him "Tuna" or "Charlie Tuna". You never lose your childhood nicknames. We had some decent ones like "Little Debbie" and "Baby Ruth".

One event that stands out in my mind (to this day) happened when I was attending Cloverdale Junior High School. We were living in southwest Little Rock on Pine Cone Drive. After what had been a normal day, my brother experienced another medical emergency. What led up to this event, I don't remember. However, I distinctly recall looking at him and crying. He had turned blue, stopped breathing, and there was absolutely nothing I could do for him. So, I stood there, frozen in place, and cried. I vowed that day I would always watch over him.

Maybe that's the reason I became an Instructor Trainer in advanced level CPR and emergency response.

(I had never made this connection before writing these words.) I did my best to keep my secret vow until I left home and eventually joined the military. Over the years, I visited him when I could. He was always happy to see me. It didn't matter where he was or how long it had been since our last visit. I always felt genuine love from him.

"I was in the middle of a bad dream . . . hoping I would wake up."

After a long while, he would move close to my older brother and me. By this time, I was out of the military, working a full-time job, and taking college classes. We'd meet up for lunch or he'd come over to my house for dinner. It seems he was always working, trying to keep his head above water. He started his own lawn care business, and I helped with flyers and business cards. I remember the first time he drove us to lunch in his pickup truck. He was so proud of his big, red Ford truck . . . but his driving scared the crap out of me! After that, I would always offer to drive (chuckle).

At one point, I was having difficulties with a relationship and my job, and money was tight. I had little back then, but I always helped my brother out as much as I could. I think his condition was worsening (even though I didn't realize it at the time). When I saw him, he would be more stressed than usual. Over time, I saw him less and less.

I couldn't handle the added drama of him being upset about life and going on rants. I knew his life was rough, but I felt there wasn't much I could do to help him.

We went out for lunch in January and it was a good day! I was so glad to spend some time with him. Our lunch lasted longer than my allotted hour, so I had to get back to work. He came into the building with me and we chatted in the foyer for a few more minutes. As he was leaving, he gave me one of his famous bear hugs. Then he said, "I love you, sis." I knew he meant those words! I told him, "I love you too, bro." and I meant every word! After he left, I went back to my cubical city job.

Often I've wondered if he knew he had little time left. Normally, he would just drop me off at work after our lunches. My lunch hour went long that day, and he also came inside to talk to me for a few more minutes. It was almost like he didn't want our time to end. I don't know. It's one of those things that comes to mind later (like flashbacks in slow motion) and you kick yourself for not having noticed. Anyway, I'm SO glad we had that lunch, talk, and a good time together that day. It was a gift from God. It was also the last time I would see my brother.

A couple of weeks later, I'm on the phone with my sister and the doorbell rang. I put the phone down and answered the door. It was my sister-in-law. I was happy to see her and smiled, but noticed she wasn't smiling back. She had a strange look on her face (and I noticed my niece had stayed in their car).

I think I asked her what was wrong. She told me my older brother had found my younger brother unresponsive at his house earlier that afternoon. The paramedics had pronounced him dead at the scene.

I remember letting out a scream, my knees buckled, and I fell to the floor sobbing. I forgot my sister was still on the phone . . . hearing my pain-filled scream. My fiancé came running into the room in a panic. It seems my sister-in-law got on the phone with my younger sister and told her what had happened. I don't remember talking to my sister again on that call. I was in the middle of a bad dream . . . hoping I would wake up.

I felt I had failed my brother. I promised to look after him and I wasn't there to help him when he needed me the most. Later, we learned my brother had a seizure and fell in such a way that he couldn't breathe. One day I was getting the bear hug and the next he was gone forever. I felt guilty because I hadn't been spending as much time with him.

The next month was a blur. My sister and youngest brother traveled in to help clean out his house. We packed up (or gave away) his stuff and made funeral arrangements. We were told (because of the autopsy) it wasn't a good idea to view his body. I felt I couldn't even say goodbye. When I saw the spot where he had fallen and died, I cried hysterically. One time, I tripped on the stairs while packing his stuff and landed on my butt.

Any will to get up left me, so I sat there and sobbed for a while.

I had offered God my life for his many times, but that's not how it works. My brother always talked about how much he wanted a wife and family. He bought his house (the one we were now packing up) to get ready for that. It's sad beyond words he didn't live long enough to do the things he wanted most in life. It utterly and completely broke my heart.

". . . after thirty-seven years, no one could save him."

When a loved one dies, it helps a great deal to recall the fun times you shared with them. Sometimes my brother would do unexpected things or say something so bizarre that you just had to laugh. Even though it might embarrass and cause unwanted attention, you still had to laugh. During this sad time of his passing, my sister-in-law shared a story about Charlie that we still laugh about today . . .

My brother was expecting an important delivery one day. The snow had piled up next to his mailbox, so the postal worker didn't stop at my brother's house. Well, when my brother saw the postal truck drive past his mailbox, he went outside and chased down the mailman!

He asked the mailman why he hadn't delivered to his house and the postman replied my brother hadn't cleared the snow from around his mailbox.

My brother told him he had cleared the snow that morning. He let him know he should have delivered his mail. At some point, my brother felt like the mail carrier was arguing with him. So, he asked him if he knew who he was. The postman said that he didn't. My brother replied, "I'm Mr. Rogers, and this is my neighborhood!" He got his mail. When I heard that story, my mouth was hanging open, and I said, "Oh, my God!", but I started laughing just the same. It was a classic Charlie situation and the first stress relief I'd had during that time.

My siblings and I loaded up Charlie's big red pickup truck and a U-Haul truck. We headed back to Arkansas on a chilly and overcast day in January. Our brother's ashes we buckled securely (next to the driver) to bring him home to our mom. Charlie was so proud of his truck. We figured we'd give him one last ride in it. It may sound silly, but those are the kind of thoughts you have when someone close to you passes away.

Not long into our journey, we hit a big snowstorm. The interstate in Wyoming shut down. We navigated back roads for hours (with white knuckles and frazzled nerves) to get out of it. Somewhere in Wyoming or Nebraska, I got pulled over in that red truck. All I remember was crying and telling the trooper I just wanted to get my brother home.

The cop shined his flashlight on the urn, cautioned me to drive safely, and let me go without a ticket.

It was a long and exhausting trip. I was relieved when I saw the Welcome to Arkansas sign, but I also dreaded what I would have to do once we got to our mom's house. Since I was the oldest child present, I felt I had to be the one to talk to my mom first. I'll never forget it as long as I live.

Once we arrived, I unstrapped my brother's urn and went into my mom's house. She was sitting at the dining table waiting for us to arrive. I said to her "Mom, we've brought your son home.", and I handed her the urn. She wasn't crying, but I was. I think she was still in shock. Maybe it was like a bad dream she couldn't wake from as well. I hugged her and said, "I'm so sorry, Momma."

I felt so bad for her. I wanted to help her feel better, but there was nothing I could do. She had rushed him to the hospital so many times. Countless times she had taken a ride with him in the back of ambulances. So many nights she had spent worrying about him . . . praying for him . . . and after thirty-seven years, no one could save him.

Arranging the service and everything that followed was a blur. I remember telling a couple of funny stories and singing *Go Rest High on That Mountain* (with some altered lyrics) at his service. Every time I looked at his photo, I cried. When I thought I couldn't possibly have any tears left, more came.

I refused to listen to his funeral song for years. I would either change the radio station or walk out of the place where it was playing. I simply couldn't hear it without breaking down in uncontrollable sobs. Such was the depth of my grief.

I don't remember what all happened after we placed his urn in the mausoleum. How I got back to Utah is a mystery to me to this day. It's almost like I just woke up one day and I was back home, some 1300 miles from Arkansas. Life was different . . . like a big ol' piece was missing. Time goes on, and you adjust to your new life without a person. (I wanted to say you get used to it, but you really don't. You just learn to go on without them.)

"Moms are like that . . . they have super-hero thoughts."

Everyone has their own time and way of grieving. For me, it went on for years. I couldn't even say his name or think of him without crying. At one point, my physician wanted to refer me to mental health because it had been four years since my brother passed and I would still sob uncontrollably. Yep, I held on to guilt for many years. That false guilt I really needed to let go. The songs he liked, places he'd been, or things he used to say would visit me at random times. One night, similar circumstances would send me into an almost full-blown mental breakdown.

My baby brother was supposed to call me one night, and he didn't. I called him several times, and it went to voice mail. After a few hours without a response, I drove to his house and knocked on the door. His truck was in the driveway. It was early evening, so I figured he wasn't asleep. I knocked on the front door and waited. Then I knocked on the back door and waited. After a few minutes, I knocked again on both doors. A panic (I wasn't consciously aware of) was building inside me. I knocked again and again with no answer. Suddenly, the building panic released like a ton of bricks! I started sobbing furiously and had to sit down on the back steps. I couldn't control it! My subconscious mind, riddled with past guilt, had gone to a dark place. A place where my baby brother lay dead inside his home . . . all alone. He had died just like my younger brother!

Shortly after I proceeded with my mental breakdown, my brother came around the corner and found me there on his steps, crying like a banshee. Poor guy, he couldn't figure out what was going on. I'm sure he thought something terrible had happened! At first, I couldn't talk. Slowly, I described to him what was going on. He did his best to understand, but I really couldn't explain it myself. My guilt over my younger brother's death had built up to a present-day flashback.

It's easy to forgive others, but much harder to forgive yourself. We usually beat ourselves up far worse than anyone else ever could.

Although there are still times when I'll cry my eyes out when I think of my brother, it's a lot easier than it was in those first eight years. I choose to remember the fun times and the crazy stuff he did. I feel deeply honored and blessed to have known and loved him for thirty-seven years.

I think it's amazing how life plays out . . . how things work in a circle. My mom never really got over the death of her son. Maybe (like me) she felt guilty. Perhaps she thought there was something she could have done to save him. It's possible she believed she could have done something different when he was growing up. Moms are like that . . . they have superhero thoughts. They have trouble realizing that sometimes nothing you could have said or done would have changed the outcome.

I think about how it all turned out and believe God gave my mom a gift. She would forget that her son had died and they would reunite some ten years later. More life happened in that space of time that needs to be told now.

What My Brother Taught Me

1. Do what makes you happy!
2. Don't be so serious all the time!
3. Regardless of your limitations, never give up or give in.
4. Love your family despite their quirks and deeds.

5. Always remember to give family members a hug and tell them you love them. Spend time with them. You never know when will be the last time you see them.
6. Never feel less than anyone else.
7. Be yourself, not what others want you to be.

The prediction of long ago came true today.
Sometimes I think I've cried all I can and still, the
tears come down like rain.

There are no words to describe the hurt my heart has
today.

No words to express the way I feel . . . but empty.

I feel the urge to mourn.
Cut my hair.
Chant my death song.
Cut until the pain is greater than the hurt in my heart.

Again I feel as yesterday, like a million tears from a
hundred forgotten nations.

I hang my head and know . . . today is a good day to
die.

10
Devastating Consequences

We never know how things are going to turn out, but now and then we see a glimpse into the future and hope it doesn't come true. Sometimes we can hope, pray, and bargain . . . all to no avail. This glance into the future was always a part of my relationship with my nephew, Ryan. It didn't show itself straight away, but I could feel it hanging around . . . waiting. Would it swoop in like an eagle catching a lake trout, unseen until the moment it strikes? Would it vanish by a last-minute decision to take a different path? I prayed for a change in direction that would make the "squatter" on the fringes of my subconscious leave forever. However, the way life played out, the eagle came instead.

I remember my nephew when he was a baby in diapers. As a toddler, he had so much energy and a desire to explore his world. His eyes were deep . . . as if they could look into your soul. Ryan's smile made people happy.

He was a cute boy who had it bad growing up. Way worse than what I'd lived through. He just wanted to be loved, explore, and have fun (like most children). I don't believe he received any of those things. Maybe in short-lived, small doses that left him wondering when (or if) he would be lucky enough to get another taste.

"No good will come of this."

I lived with my older sister (his mom) for a couple of years while finishing high school. I had no other place to go. My sister didn't care about doing much around the house and had a wicked temper. It wasn't really that different from my early days growing up with an alcoholic father. My nephew and I were always walking on eggshells so we wouldn't wake her up or incur her wrath some other way. Going to school was my only respite from the demented drama in her house. I also became the maid, cook, clothes washer, and mandatory source of additional income. I did whatever I thought would keep the drama to a minimum.

Drama, it seems, came regularly despite my best efforts to keep it at a minimum. There were days I'd come home, and she'd be going off the rails about my nephew getting out of the house while she was sleeping. It was my fault (of course). Or maybe he ate something she didn't want him to eat. I mean, it was pretty much "pick any excuse" for her to fly into a rage and beat on a toddler.

My nephew was her "punching bag". My sister didn't have an "off switch" for her rage. By the time I got home, Ryan would have belt welts all over him or red marks where she'd slapped him hard. Many times, those welts and red marks turned into deep bruises. Sometimes his skin was open and bleeding from whatever she hit him with. I was in a pickle because I had nowhere else to live and didn't want to leave my nephew there alone.

One day, I called Child Protective Services (CPS) about the abuse and neglect going on in the home. This was difficult for me because she was my sister. CPS announced their visit ahead of time (which I never understood). Before their visit, my sister cleaned the house from top to bottom. When the social worker arrived, everything appeared normal and my sister answered her questions with stories meant to elicit sympathy. My sister didn't take any responsibility for her choices or actions. She blamed me, my nephew, his father, and the nosey neighbors. Not a thing changed from that CPS visit, except life became more difficult for me and my nephew.

It was a few months later when a neighbor called CPS again. They again announced when they were coming and the same scene played out. After one particularly terrible event, I called them again, and this time they let slip that I had made the call!

I was thinking, "Thanks a lot for pointing me out, knowing I live in the same house!"

Things became tense around the house once CPS could make unannounced visits. I think it was the only thing holding Ryan's mom in check. They also gave my sister a list of things she had to do, including counseling. The social worker starting stopping by more frequently because my sister wasn't going to her mandated counseling appointments. When she asked my sister why she wasn't keeping her appointments, my sister had a list of excuses. Some excuses were not having a car, no money for a taxi, too far to walk, no one to give her a ride, or her ride didn't show up. I don't think she ever intended to go to those counseling appointments. She was just biding her time with the "poor me" act.

A few months after another call for help went sideways, I graduated from high school and joined the military. Pulling both off was nothing short of a miracle. My life had been a shit storm for years. I hung in there despite the challenges and used a "hail Mary" pass to break free from it. On the day I left for basic training, I gave my nephew a hug, told him I loved him, and said goodbye. I felt compelled to look at him one last time before I got into the car to leave. As I did, time slowed down, and I heard, "No good will come of this." It made me sad.

It frustrated me I wasn't able to help him get out of that environment. I had no job, no home, and nothing to offer. My plan was to spend two years in the military and then file for custody of him.

His life would change, and I would have removed him from his abusive environment. But, as they say, the best-laid plans seldom work out the way we envision them.

> *"I felt like I was in some horrible night-mare and asked God, "Please, wake me up! Please!", but I WAS awake."*

After spending three years overseas, the Air Force sent me to Arizona. This was about twenty hours from home. My sister had moved to another town about two hours away from the family. Then one day I got the news they had vanished! Simply disappeared, telling no one where they had gone. They were nowhere to be found when relatives searched for them. My family was concerned for the safety of the children. All of us were in a state of shock mixed with fear and helplessness.

My head filled with scary thoughts. Had their mom been kidnapped or killed? Did she move away with some guy we didn't know about? Were they all dead, buried some place where they'd never be found? These are the thoughts going through your head when something like this happens. I'm guessing we didn't have money to pay for a private investigator. I wasn't able to help the rest of the family look for them. It seems my family looked for a long time and finally didn't know what else to do.

Looking back, this event sparked my interest in finding missing persons (and giving the names back to unidentified remains) around the world.

About eight years later, I was visiting my aunt, and she confessed to me she had known all along where my nephew was! She told me she was sworn to secrecy (by my sister) or else all communication would stop. She hadn't said a word because she didn't want to lose contact completely. The range of emotions I felt upon learning that BIG FREAKIN' CHUNK OF INFORMATION was hard to describe. Somewhere between relief, anger, and confusion would have been close. I didn't understand. It was like some crazy-ass drama you see on TV! Really? I felt happy because at least he was still alive. For years, the family had doubted that.

Apparently, my sister started getting into trouble with CPS in the small town they'd moved to prior to their disappearing act. Fearing legal action, my sister moved to another state where there wasn't a pile of evidence against her. Maybe it was like a self-imposed clean slate move. Later we learned this new state started getting complaints too . . . lots of them. The rest of the family didn't seem surprised at these reports.

I felt guilty also, like I had caused the disappearing act. It seems this type of guilt comes readily to those who grow up around such chaos. I knew my sister totally hated my guts at that point, but I think the part I played in it all was small.

I carried that guilt for quite a few years, though. Life went on. There was nothing I could do to repair or change our relationship. About ten years after her vanishing act, the eagle waiting on the fringes of my subconscious came swooping in. It was a fast dive (only taking seconds), accomplished with pinpoint accuracy, leaving devastation in its wake.

I received a call from my younger sister telling me my nephew had been arrested and charged with two counts of capital murder! This news came so far from left field I couldn't grasp it. It was like my brain couldn't process the information. My knees went weak, and I felt like someone had punched me in the stomach while sitting on my chest. The slow-motion vision and message I'd heard (when he was a child) came back. The scene played repeatedly in my mind. I couldn't wrap my head around the immensity of it all. I cried for days and tried grasping onto some little straw of reality. Surely this could not be!

An investigator came to town and talked with family members about Ryan's child abuse. He wanted us to testify for the defense. My mom never testified on behalf of my nephew. When the investigator questioned her, she acted like she couldn't remember any details. I'm not sure why she did it. Maybe she didn't want to betray her daughter as I had. Perhaps she wanted to avoid feeling shame for having done nothing to stop the abuse. She was the one who knew everything!

I remember sitting there, a shocked look on my face, as she lied about her memories of the abuse. Okay, maybe she didn't lie, but she pretended like she couldn't remember, so . . . It pissed me off, and I stayed mad at her for a while over it. Shortly after sitting down with the investigator, my sister and I were on planes headed to a capital trial, in a state that's proud of their death penalty, and carries out said punishment on the regular.

Once we arrived, we were told the complete story of what happened. We were told our testimony was part of the penalty phase of the trial. My nephew had already been tried and found guilty of one count of capital murder! (We hadn't known about the trial because we still didn't know where my sister had taken her kids. This is how we found out!)

I cried for the victims and what happened that day. It was beyond sad that my nephew never had a chance at life. The crime scene photos were ghastly. It was obvious the paramedics tried desperately to save one victim. Such heroic actions weren't necessary for the second victim, who died instantly. My tears flowed for those poor souls who were just going about their life. They had no warning of the chaos, fear, and suffering that awaited them that day. I felt like I was in some horrible nightmare and asked God, "Please, wake me up! Please!", but I WAS awake.

Now I've lived through people hating me because of my skin color, but I'm here to tell you . . . it's nothing compared to the raw hate coming from the people in that courtroom and local community. I could only imagine their pain, and I understood why they directed it at just about anyone who gave them a reason . . . but I still wondered, "Why me?"

I wasn't the one who harmed their family! I hadn't said a word against them and cried for the victims! Wishing it all undone couldn't make it so. Even the police, prosecutor, and jailers treated me with disdain. It was almost like they were pissed at me for having the audacity to try to save my nephew from what they saw as his "just" punishment. I certainly got a "belly full" of that state.

"Murder has a rippling effect. Like a stone thrown into a calm lake, the ripples travel outward (in all directions) as far as the eye can see."

Anyway, I testified about everything I knew about Ryan's life. My intention was to paint a picture (for the jury) of what he had to endure during his brief life. I hoped a first-hand account of the abuse and neglect he suffered would spare his life. Afterward, I left the courtroom and went somewhere to sit and just exploded into body-shuddering sobs I could not control.

My face was wet, snot was pouring from my nose, and I was wailing to the heavens. All the past reared its ugly head. All the pain, sorrow, failure, loss, and helplessness rode on those tears. My sister could not console me and passersby took a wide berth.

Once I went back into the courtroom, I listened to more testimony. Experts, teachers, child protection agencies, and more that I cannot recall, spoke about the years of abuse the children suffered. After all the testimony concluded, the judge sent the jury out to deliberate. The story had been told . . . both versions of it. The twelve people now locked in a room had to make one of the hardest decisions of their lives. I did not envy them!

Once the jury had reached a verdict, the news spread like a wildfire and all parties made their way back to the courtroom. It was hard to sit there, hold in my emotions, and wait for the sentence to be read. The judge warned onlookers against any outbursts in his court. I noticed some jurors were crying. The jury foreman handed the decision to the bailiff, who handed it to the judge. The judge read the decision, then instructed the defendant (my nephew) to rise and read the sentence aloud. Death by lethal injection was the penalty for the crime committed. The family of the victims cried tears of joy because justice had been served. Our family cried tears of grief. Although we had told the horrible story of what our nephew went through in his brief life, we were unsuccessful in having his life spared.

After the sentencing phase of the trial concluded, I visited my nephew in the county jail. I hadn't seen him in about fifteen years. He looked like a grown man! We talked through a thick, plastic type of cell. I told him I loved him. He was happy to see me! He still had those deep eyes and a catching smile . . . although a sad one. I think he was grateful that I tried to help him once again. I don't recall how long I was in that dreadful place, but I remember feeling this overwhelming urge to leave as quickly as possible.

Before all this happened, I had a long-held belief in the death penalty. During this trial, I questioned this and a lot of other beliefs I held. I was baptized in a Southern Baptist church, believed in God and his son Jesus, and in the "Word of God". While this was going on, God asked me, "How can you believe in *The Holy Bible* and still have this belief?" I contemplated that question and The Ten Commandments for a while. I realized my belief in the commandments left no room for my death penalty belief. Some laws are manmade disguised as something else. I remembered many Bible verses during those days and released this belief I once held as truth.

This realization of my faith didn't come lightly. This event forever changed me. It strengthened me and my faith. People whose families have never been touched by murder don't realize its far-reaching effects. They don't see how it devastates the families on both sides.

They are blind to how it physically, emotionally, and psychologically affects everyone who has anything to do with the case or trial.

We cannot know how hearing the testimony (and seeing all the crime scene photos) affected the twelve people on the jury, the families, the onlookers, or the press. It may affect them to this day. Each one of the jurors passed a death sentence. Can we even fathom how doing that affected each of them?

I learned something else about our judicial system as well. I went into the process believing (naively) I'd find out the truth about what happened. Not if it had happened, but how it had happened. How did the whole situation play out? Why did things go sideways so fast? Why did he make those choices instead of others? I suppose I wanted these answers because I still couldn't wrap my head around the enormity of it all. I had hoped that the justice system would help me grasp it. Yet here's what happened . . .

The defense had their story and evidence for it, and the prosecution had their story and evidence for it. His jury simply looked at and weighed the evidence given by both sides and determined if the evidence proved "beyond a reasonable doubt" his guilt or innocence. I believe only the people there when it happened know exactly how everything went down. Everything else is theory, forensic evidence and re-creation, witness testimony, and expert testimony to back up (or debunk) the evidence presented.

One of my observations about crime and the judicial system is NO ONE touched by it is ever the same! Murder has a rippling effect. Like a stone thrown into a calm lake, the ripples travel outward (in all directions) as far as the eye can see.

After all was said and done, I flew back home, but it didn't seem like home anymore. Something was missing . . . different. It felt like a big ol' hole right through the middle of me. For years, I would carry that hole around with me. Before I testified at the trial, I had been nicotine free for ten years. I lit up my first cigarette in a decade at the courthouse. I didn't bring any home with me, but about two weeks later, I walked into a store and bought a pack. Little did I know, but starting smoking again would benefit me a few years later, when I had to go back to that dreadful place and testify again.

"Suddenly I felt a deep sense of peace unlike any I'd ever known."

Yep, I went back for my nephew's second trial and gave my testimony again. I didn't want to go, but knew they would serve me with a subpoena if I didn't. The second trial was like reliving the first one (ever watch the movie Groundhog Day?). I felt better prepared because I understood the process. Being still numb from the first trial, I didn't lose my mind. I cried, but mostly felt defeated, like I had helped check off a box on some legal "to do" list.

I didn't feel anyone gave a shit. I felt they just wanted what they wanted and wouldn't settle for less. My efforts resulted in the same verdict and sentence as the first trial. I went back home and wondered if the court helped families pay for counseling. I felt like I needed it, so I saw a counselor for a while. It helped. Life still felt weird, but I started getting on with it.

Have you ever played a song repeatedly for months? The song for me was *Long December* by Counting Crows. I listened to that song hundreds of times after the first trial: "And it's been a long December and there's reason to believe maybe this year will be better than the last." I'm sure the lyrics aren't even about what I was making them about, but it stuck like Chuck (maybe because the first trial was in December).

For months and months, I listened to that song and sang along. I was crying most of those times, but it helped me feel better. Then suddenly, one day, I was good . . . done. Since then, I've only occasionally listened to that song. It seemed to be part of my therapy. I've always liked all kinds of music and enjoyed dancing. I think *Long December* was a gift from God (or the angels) to help me through that rough time. A few years later, God and the angels helped me with my nephew again. This time it was to help him go Home.

I'd been learning about my Indian heritage and wanted to help my nephew cross over easily.

I was worried that maybe his fear of death or the lethal injection process would make his spirit hesitate or something and he'd be "stuck" here somehow. In other words, I was concerned for his soul after all that had happened. So I decided I would do a ceremony for him.

Basically, that meant spending four days without food, praying for him, and envisioning him going into The Light. Regardless of what people believe about God, I'd like to think we all want people to go where they're supposed to go when they die. (I don't want spirits hanging out where they're not supposed to be.)

So I fasted, prayed, and dreamed . . . over and over. I sent him thoughts of love, shared my memories of him, and my sadness about how things turned out. When his execution day came, I didn't know what time it would happen. I stayed in my Sacred Circle, called in the horses to give him a swift ride to the Other Side, and drifted in and out of consciousness. Suddenly, I felt a deep sense of peace unlike any I'd ever known. I noted the time on the clock. He was gone, and I knew it, felt it. I started crying and grieving for a long while. It seemed to me a most wicked way to die.

After a while, I got up off the floor and realized how weak I'd become. I heated some broth and sipped it slowly, calming myself as I thought about what had just transpired.

Realizing God and the angels helped me to know he was safely on the Other Side, so I wouldn't worry anymore. I felt blessed and grateful for the divine help and the reminder that God does indeed answer prayers.

"And just like that, the little boy with deep eyes and an infectious smile was no more."

Later, I logged onto the Department of Corrections website for news on death sentences carried out that day. I found and read the story about his execution. The reporter listed the time they pronounced my nephew dead. It was the exact time I had noted when the feeling of peace came over me. Some people don't believe things like this can happen, yet they believe in God. I've never understood that. If a person believes that God (or Jesus) is all-knowing and all-powerful, how can this be impossible? Perhaps that's the difference between disbelief and belief . . . when one experiences it for themselves. I experienced it, so I know it happened and is possible.

The song that stuck in my mind after his passing was *The Only One* by Tracy Chapman. "Together, oh together, no, there'll be no more of that. Sometimes I hear her calling straight from the house of God. I've mostly lost the voice to speak, and any words to say except, does heaven have enough angels yet?" It was a while before this song left me also, but it did.

I've seldom listened to it over the years until writing this chapter.

All the worry, fear, drama, hope, and heartbreak concluded with my nephew leaving this world. It's strange how his mother forged him into what he became, yet she never faced the justice system for her part. I cried the day I crossed out his address in my address book. And just like that (finger snap), the little boy with deep eyes and an infectious smile was no more. I've wondered if his disregard for human life stemmed from being shown his life didn't matter for all those years. If we don't experience love growing up, it seems we lack capacity for it. I don't have those answers, but my love for him is still strong and I'm glad he's getting all the love in heaven he so desperately sought in life.

The weight of all that had happened sat heavily on my shoulders for years. I carried grief and guilt over his loss for a long time. Eventually, I realized I had done my best to create a detour for him to take and rewrite his life story. In time, I started feeling stronger, had more energy, and was happy again! My period of happiness was short-lived before the next chapter of this decades-old drama unfolded.

What my Nephew Taught Me

1. Whatever you may have done in your life, there is forgiveness (if you seek it), and a place in hell isn't yours (unless you choose it).

2. God will always bring His children back Home if they so wish it.
3. Believing in something doesn't make it The Truth. Our beliefs are our truth.
4. Think carefully about what you do before you do it. YOU CANNOT FATHOM the effects it will have.
5. If you take someone's life, you rob them of their chance to live their purpose in this life.

It feels good to be home, but I find it's not home anymore.
Not quite.

Something is different.
Like something missing or something acquired that doesn't fit.

An emptiness.
A loneliness.
A sense of loss.

Perhaps it is me feeling as I do.
Like a stranger to myself and all that is around me.

Not knowing from where it came.
Not knowing how to give it back.
Feeling so tired from all the years.

The past has returned.
Reminding me of its misery.

Of the need to stop the cycle.
Of the long, long road ahead.

11
Death From the Inside Out

Childhood memories of my older sister Lyn are few. Maybe because it's been a long time since our childhood. She was five years older than me. We didn't have the same friends or go to the same schools for long. To me, my sister was always sad. Maybe our home life (along with the racism, bullying, and school fights) made her sad. If I were to guess, I'd say all the siblings were sad kids. When you're young, you don't notice how sad you are, but you can see it in other people's eyes or their face shows it. I remember, like me, my sis loved spending time on my grandparent's farm.

We all worked hard on the farm, but it made us feel alive and gave us a sense of belonging. It kept the family working together, food on the table, and ensured there was enough firewood to make it through the winter. One blessing from spending time on the farm was the hassles of inner-city and home-life drama disappeared.

The farm was the only place where we got a breather from the chaos and abuse in our lives. We all seemed a lot happier there. If we had our choice, we would have just stayed there to grow up. Given the choice, we would have lived there forever, but that's not how our life stories were written.

My sister and I grew up with the same dad until my mom divorced him when I was in elementary school. Lyn had different physical features and a different last name than her siblings. As kids, we didn't notice stuff like that. We were all family. In her early teens, Lyn was told about her biological dad. Our aunt revealed who her real dad was and what had happened between him and our mom. Things went downhill after that.

"A sense of relief washed over us once we knew we each shared the same secret."

I can't say the exact day it happened, but my sister started acting differently, getting into trouble and running away. Her behavior got so bad they sent her to a juvenile girl's home in Pine Bluff, Arkansas. She came back home after a few months, but she was different somehow. I don't think the juvenile home helped her much. It seemed like she was worse off instead of rehabilitated. Maybe she suffered abuse while she was there (like so many youths we hear about on the news or social media). What really happened there? No one can say for sure.

I don't remember her ever talking about it. I know life didn't improve for her, me, or my baby sister after that.

Not long after my sister returned home, my mom found another man she thought she would marry. Her fiancee became the reason we felt afraid to go to sleep at night. We didn't understand what was happening at first. He would sneak into our rooms after everyone was asleep. We would wake up and he'd be standing in our room . . . staring at us. We were terrified every night we would wake up with a hand fondling our private parts. He'd leave the room quickly if we woke up. Sometimes I wonder if this was to confuse us, so we thought we had dreamed the whole thing.

These insights into our collective torture were in hindsight. We each thought we were the only one experiencing the nightly stalking. Not sure how my other sisters handled his "visits", but I tried my best to stay awake every night! I guess I thought it would be safer if I could stay awake. But I couldn't outlast the night creeper. It seems I also tucked my blankets in tight around me so I'd wake up before he could get his hands near my private parts. Waking up with him standing in my room, staring at me, stayed with me for years. Out of all the perverted things he did, how his face would change into creepy when he stared at me haunted me the most.

Our pedophile's first name was Jim. I think his last name was Brown, but I'm uncertain.

The tidbits of information I remember from childhood seem weird and arbitrary. Like, I remember his first name, that he was chubby, and he drove a gold-brown Mercury Cougar. If I were to guess his type, it would be young girls between the ages of eight and thirteen based on how old we were when the molestation started.

One day (out of the blue), my sister's and I started talking about the night creeper we had in common. I don't remember what sparked the conversation. I guess we had kept our individual secret because of the feelings we didn't know what to do with. A sense of relief washed over us once we knew we each shared the same secret. We were afraid to tell our mom about our abuser (but even more afraid of keeping it secret). We stuck together (like *The Three Musketeers*) to tell our mom what had been going on while she slept.

All hell broke loose after our sit-down with Mom (as you can imagine). She kicked his sorry ass to the curb that very day! Our lives had changed forever (although we didn't know it at the time), but we solved that HUGE problem together with courage and strength! After feeling weak and helpless for so long, we felt empowered! It was proof positive we were going to become strong women. I was proud of my sisters that day (and still am). It's sad to say, but this was also the time I felt closest to my older sister. Strange how things get categorized in our minds. That powerful time is how I choose to remember my older sister.

Once we got through the drama with our mom's fiancé, I didn't see my sister much. It's like she faded from my memory somehow. The last time I remember her living with us was after my mom kicked the pervert out. I remember the little house we lived in on Pine Cone Drive in southwest Little Rock. It seems my sister ran away from there and never came back. Maybe it was the molester dude that made her leave. I don't know, but who could blame her?

"Yep, I threw the daddy card right in his face."

Confessions are a powerful thing. I must confess that once I found out the pedophile had molested my little sister, anger started building in me. It's weird, but I wasn't angry about what he did to me. I guess I felt I was old enough to deal with it, but my little sister? Maybe the need to protect my siblings kicked in again. Who knows? Even though my mom had kicked him out, this didn't soothe the growing anger within my heart. I wanted him to go to jail, but he didn't for whatever reason. Over time, my anger grew into hate. My hate turned into vengeance.

One night I talked my best friend into finding us a ride to go look for "the creeper". It was my sole intent to find him and kill him. He deserved to die for what he did to my baby sister! I told myself if I didn't kill him, he would do it again and again if allowed to live.

It's the only time in my life I remember feeling so much anger and hate. If I had found him that night, I would have killed him (or died trying). How is it that a young girl is driven to kill?

It's been many years and I'm sure he's dead by now. I can only hope he didn't continue to molest little girls for the rest of his life. Looking back, I'm glad I didn't find him. If I had killed him, my life would have turned out completely different from how it did, and this book never written. I believe this was yet another case of divine intervention on my behalf.

The story of how me and my sister reconnected after many years is bizarre (like so many things in my life). It all started with my stepdad and a pot of coffee.

After several years, my mom remarried. My stepdad and I didn't get along well. He was an okay man, but sometimes he'd talk down to me. I think we sort of tolerated each other. Both of us were stuck in the same situation and tried to make the best of it. One day (when I was around sixteen), a weird thing happened. He told me (in his condescending tone of voice), to make him some coffee. It wasn't an ask, but a tell (like ordering me around). So, for whatever reason, I decided I wasn't making him a single drop of coffee unless he asked me nicely (guess I'd reached my "max fill" level).

He returned a few minutes later and asked why I hadn't made coffee. I told him because he was being mean and didn't ask.

He repeated his order (this time it was to make him some damn coffee now). I told him I would be happy to make his coffee if he would ask nicely. He just said I'd better do what I was told and went back outside. Well, that did it! My stubbornness kicked in and I became a snapping turtle, bit down on it, and wasn't letting go.

After a while, he came back inside, looking for his cup of coffee. (It wasn't there.) He raised his voice, asking me why I couldn't do what I was told. I said in a calm voice, "Why can't you ask me nicely and not curse?" It seems I followed that up with, "If you can't be nice, then you can make your own coffee." His reply was, "I told you to do it, and you're going to make the damn coffee!" Then I went there . . . yep, I threw the daddy card right in his face! I said, "You're not my daddy! You can't tell me what to do!"

My mom walked into the room just as I played the daddy card. She didn't hear the way he'd been talking to me, only what I had said. She asked me what I was doing talking to my dad that way. My blood was getting pretty warm, and I tried to explain how he was treating me. She sided with him and told me I'd best do what I was told. I stepped way out on the edge of backtalk and told her, "All he has to do is ask nicely and I will make the coffee." My stepdad was steaming hot by now. He didn't say a word, but my mom told me to make his coffee. When I refused, she kicked me out of the house on the spot. Boom! Just like that!

I suppose it shouldn't have shocked me since it had happened a few years prior. On that occasion, I wandered around (and slept outside) for a few days before being allowed to come back home. This time, the shock and hurt hit me hard because my mom took his side over mine. She knew he was a condescending ass, but chose him over her own flesh and blood. I learned two lessons that day. First, once I've made up my mind, that's it. I'm like a dog on a bone. Second, a lack of respect brings immediate negative consequences.

"No one was listening to my cries for help."

I stayed with a friend for a few days before becoming homeless for a short time. Somehow I ended up moving in with my older sister (I'm not sure how the arrangement came about). Maybe my mom had talked to her about helping me out. I'm sure my stepdad didn't want me back in their house. We rubbed each other the wrong way too much for his taste. Perhaps having one less mouth to feed was a relief as well. Who knows? I was glad to have a roof over my head and another shot at finishing high school.

When I moved in with my sister, she had one child she'd had before turning eighteen. So, it was me, her, and my two-year-old nephew living in a small, two-bedroom mobile home.

Four months before I moved out and joined the military, she would give birth to her second son. The already cramped trailer would become an even more drama-filled hell hole. This situation became one of the most trying periods of my life.

Living with my sister was like traveling back in time to the home we'd grown up in, only worse! I know . . . unbelievable! As mentioned in the previous chapter, she expected me to babysit, clean the house, do laundry, and run errands. Going to school, working part-time, and paying most of my earnings to my sister for rent rounded out my mandatory responsibilities. The cherry on top was enduring verbal and emotional abuse and witnessing the severe physical abuse and neglect of my nephew.

More times than I can count, I thought I would not make it. Not being able to graduate high school was also a genuine fear. Most days I felt stuck in some hellish nightmare I couldn't wake up from. Moving back in with my mom wasn't an option (they had moved to another state). Things just kept going downhill. Each day seemed to bring some new drama I had to deal with.

One night I got in trouble with the law by riding along with somebody I shouldn't have. This person broke the law (okay, maybe a few) and there I was . . . at the scene of the crime as it all went down. I did nothing illegal, but I was there. After the first incident, the person driving the car we were in tried to outrun the cops using back roads.

He pulled over after a few minutes. Everyone bailed out and hid from the cops. The police were unamused and brought in the K-9 dogs to search for us. I'm not sure why the dogs didn't find me, but I got arrested at school a couple of days later. I went before the judge and he sentenced me to like five years' probation.

The negative in my life was cascading out of control. I felt like I might go crazy from the stress. Have you ever wondered, "What else could go wrong that hasn't already?" Do yourself a favor, never ask that question (because you REALLY don't want to know the answer)! Trust me. After I asked that question, both my grandparents died within two months of each other. I don't think my brain had time to process these events, much less grieve. My grieving process was releasing a little here and there. Eventually (some 15 years later), I would release the rest of it. At this moment in my life, I was a walking shell of a human, just going through the motions.

At some point I realized I HAD to graduate from high school. Fear was growing in me that if I didn't leave Arkansas, I'd just die. Flashes of my future life (described in an earlier chapter) kept coming fast and furious. Subconsciously, I knew I was getting close to my tipping point. I wasn't able to do much for my nephew. No one was listening to my cries for help. My only chance for a good life was to move out of her place, find a job, save some money, and try to adopt my nephew. The story didn't write itself that way, though.

As you know, I got out of Arkansas, found a decent job, and my plan to adopt my nephew ended when my sister disappeared with her children a few years later.

"I wished I could burn it to the ground!"

The next time I laid eyes on my sister was during the week-long penalty phase of my nephew's criminal trial. (I described this in the previous chapter.) During this time, my sister refused to see me or talk to me. She wouldn't allow me to come into her house to talk with my niece. I think she blamed me for all her problems with CPS. I don't believe she had a clue how hard it was for me to turn her in. It broke my heart because she was family, but I couldn't bear to witness the mistreatment of the children.

Fifteen years later, another chapter in this decades-old drama began. Doctors diagnosed my sister with end-stage cancer after a coworker found her unresponsive in her home. I hoped I could see her and somehow reconcile the past. She refused when I asked to see her. I prayed for her healing and the healing of the past.

When I got the news of her passing, I was at work. Her cancer had progressed beyond treatable and my sister died about two months after her diagnosis. I remember crying out and my knees going weak. My tears just kept flowing for a while. Another coworker had to drive me the two hours home.

My sister told her son she didn't want me at her funeral service. So, like my father, it had been years since I had seen her and wasn't able to start the normal grieving process. I think our siblings are a part of us, even if we aren't getting along. When they die, a piece of us that was connected to them goes missing. It's like there's a hole in the quilt of your life. You can mend it, but it will always be just a patch. It's never whole or complete again.

Just a few days after her death, I would have a spiritual experience involving my sister. She said she understood why I did what I did and also apologized for being so bullheaded. Her revealing there was nothing I could have done to save my nephew's life gave me relief. She said everything was in divine order and not to blame myself. My sister told me she loved me and mentioned the song *We Are Family* by Sister Sledge.

You may not believe in such things, but I believe when we need to know stuff for our own healing (and theirs), God makes stuff happen. A couple of weeks after my sister died, the song *Photograph* by Nickelback started playing on the radio. I burst into tears and had to pull off the road. Right there, in that parking lot, I had a spontaneous grieving session for my sister. I think she sent it to me because she was also sad about how things were between us in the end.

I don't pretend to know all the stuff my sister went through. It seems she never got over the secret revealed to her when she was a teenager.

Maybe it made her question her whole concept of who she was, what she believed, and her trust in others. Maybe it's why she started running away and other things. When I see her again, I'll ask her about this stuff, but until then I'd only be guessing. Right now we're cool, and stuff has worked itself out, so I'm good with it.

It seems sad to me that the life of my sister filled so few pages in this book. So much loss, pain, loneliness, and grief. If things were different, I'm sure I could have written an entire book about her life. Tears fill my eyes now when I see how little space she ended up occupying in my life . . . but how big the emptiness is from it.

Recently, I took a trip back to the places I had grown up. The apartment complex where we lived when I still played Cowboys and Indians was gone. Only the footprint remained. The woods (where I'd spent so many hours running and playing) were gone, replaced by buildings. Time had taken its toll on the little house on Pine Cone Drive. The mobile home on Barwood Circle was still there, but it was being used as a storage shed instead of a home. As I looked at it (in total disbelief it was still standing), I wished I could burn it to the ground! If I did, I would feel better, but it wouldn't erase or heal all that happened there, no matter how I wished it could have.

What My Sister Taught Me

1. Children are the most precious asset we have. Protect them and teach them well.

2. Whatever you create, do it with passion. Put your heart into it. (My sister was an amazing artist.)

3. Drugs don't make the sucky stuff go away. It's still there waiting for you to fix it, so fix it.

4. Forgive others . . . but most importantly, forgive yourself!

5. Any negativity you harbor for yourself or others will eat you up from the inside out.

6. Be grateful for what others give you out of the kindness of their hearts.

7. No one owes you a living. You owe it to yourself.

8. How you keep your house and yourself is how you feel about yourself and your life.

I do not wish to go back.
For there is nothing there.

Yet I'm not going forward.
Which is the source of my pain.

I read the stories of old.
My heart is homesick.

I've still to find the path.
That leads me to Home.

12
Helping Mom Go Home

W hen we're young, we vacillate between being totally dependent on our parents and demanding independence. As teenagers, we think we're so smart, have it all figured out, and believe we're untouchable (The Invincibility Fable). Once we're in our mid-twenties, we realize (in the scheme of things) we really don't know shit. Yeah, we may be good at faking it with our friends, but when we're alone, the truth sits with us.

"Yeah, our relationship was a shit-show starring two freaking idiots."

We spend years thinking our parents are old farts, behind the times, or outdated. It may seem like they are living in some other world. We disregard their advice and pay the price for lessons learned. Around our mid-thirties, we realize the adults in our life were right about a lot of stuff.

Sometimes we realize we're a lot like them. (Have you ever seen your mom or dad staring back at you when you look in the mirror?) I know, it's scary, right? Whether the adults in our lives were good or bad, they taught us lots of stuff. Maybe they taught us what NOT to do or how we shouldn't act.

Do you remember how your parents always knew everything you were up to? You thought you were so good at hiding it until you got busted. I spent many years disagreeing, staying silent, or engaging in outright defiance. I was kicked out of my mom's house twice growing up (once for something I didn't do). Were you ever punished for someone else's lie, even when you told the truth? I had a sore spot with my mom over that one for a while. The second time was for the blatant disrespect I mentioned earlier. Some parents threaten to kick their children out if they don't follow the rules. I doubt most parents actually follow up on those threats.

That certainly wasn't the case with my mom! As soon as I stepped over the line . . . out I went! It was a hard lesson I only had to learn twice. When I found my ass sleeping outside or in a ladies' bathroom, I quickly learned about not breaking rules. Kids today get away with things that previous generations wouldn't tolerate. Parents give them practically anything they want (that they don't need). Most don't have to work for them, and may view them as an entitlement. They may even grow up believing everyone owes them a living.

I guess with my mom having six kids, there had to be rules, or else she would go crazy.

I never returned after the last time my mom kicked me out. I spent years trying to make my mom proud of me (which never seemed to work). She always seemed to critique my life. When I married young, it was partly because she was so against it. Heart-to-heart conversations with her were almost non-existent and frustrated me to no end. She once said she had a mind not speak to me for five years. I replied, "Okay, fine." and hung up on her. I spent the next five years avoiding her. Eventually, my practice of sending her cards or gifts ended because she wouldn't even respond to them.

Yeah, our relationship was a shit-show starring two freaking idiots. Eventually, I decided if she wanted to make the first move; I was open to talking. I was tired of the drama and just wanted peace. After a time she started trying and I did too. I forced myself to be nice when I was around her. The entire relationship felt like something stuck up my bum that made my spine stiffen. I could only take her in small doses.

When we're in our early to mid-forties, we learn the art of stepping back and looking at life from someone else's point of view. By the time we're in our forties, we've experienced enough crap that we understand some stuff about our parents and other family members.

If we're smart, we realize being right doesn't lower our blood pressure, lessen the drama, or leave us surrounded by people who love us when we're old.

"That Barney Fife is always so funny!"

It took years for me to fully understand these lessons. At some point, you get a clue or you don't. My mom and I had been through a lot of crap. Our relationship wasn't the greatest, but I still moved back home when she got sick. Why, you may ask? My brother and sister needed help to take care of her and she's my mom despite all the other stuff. Also, I didn't want us to be sideways when she passed. Yep, there was a little selfishness on my part. Having known the guilt and unrelenting grief of words unsaid, and deeds undone, I would not go through it again. I would heal and say my piece even if the other party didn't.

About five years after I moved back to Arkansas, my mom passed away. Her body shut down because of advanced Alzheimer's and dementia. We watched her slowly deteriorate before our eyes. Watching events unfold (and not being able to do anything about them) is the worst. Her disease made her slowly forget everything she'd ever known.

My mom's life memories were the first to fade. In the end-stage, she forgot how to walk, talk, drink, eat, swallow, go to the bathroom and breathe.

In some ways, it seemed a kinder death, because she didn't know she didn't remember, and her mind was stuck in a happier time in her life. The times when her grandkids were young, her mom and dad were still alive, and none of her children or grandchildren had died.

She would tell me stories of those times like they had happened yesterday. It was hard to act like I hadn't heard them before. Sometimes she would tell a story I hadn't heard before. I wasn't sure if those stories were true or just happy imaginings of days past. The hardest times for me were when she forgot my name, her firstborn passed and I couldn't tell her, all the trips to the emergency room, and the Barney Fife Day.

The Barney Fife Day came a few days after they had rushed her to the emergency room because her kidneys were failing. The doctors rehydrated her, got the infection under control, pumped her full of nutrients, and changed the medications she was on. A couple of days later, I went to visit her at the nursing home and she was awake, alert, sitting up, a smile on her face, and talking to another lady!

The Andy Griffith Show was on TV, and Barney Fife was acting goofy as usual. I asked her if she liked the show and she said, "That Barney Fife is always so funny!" I asked her if she knew her name. With a big smile on her face, she told me her name was Mary Sue! She hadn't known her name for some time and I was floored. For a long time, she had been listless and immobile.

She still didn't know who I was. It felt like I was in an episode of *The Twilight Zone*. I sat with her for a while (enjoying her moment of clarity), then went out to my car and cried.

"I was saying . . . Hang on Momma, I'm coming!"

When I visited her a few days later, she was back to being bedridden and incoherent. Once again, I thought I might lose my mind. Was I on a virtual reality ride that transported me in and out of alternate universes or timelines? Nothing was making sense. I was simply a spectator, powerless to affect any change or ultimate outcome. After that visit, I sat in my car and cried again. I texted my sister and told her I didn't know how much more I could handle. My brain wasn't adjusting to this extended rollercoaster ride that I'd been on for over five years.

After her latest trip to the ER, her doctor recommended we consider putting her in hospice. He told us it was only a matter of time, and nothing more could be done. We contemplated the choices (and their consequences) for about two weeks. During that time, we realized we had been carrying around the false hope she would get better. None of us wanted her to continue suffering. Maybe we didn't want our own agony and helplessness to continue, either.

Placing someone into hospice is a life-altering decision with no "take backs". When all was said and done, we moved her to hospice care.

Once our mother was placed in hospice, we knew she didn't have long to live. We contacted family members and encouraged them to stop by for a last visit with her. It was a Thursday morning when the hospice nurse called to inform me that my mom had little time left. I left work and spent the afternoon and early evening with her. The rest of the day, I talked to her and cried. I surrounded her with a pink light to let her know we loved her. Asking the angels to help her go quickly to The Light. Her breathing was labored. I couldn't do anything except watch it happen. At one point, I felt Archangel Azrael's (Angel of Death) presence and our Ancestors coming to The Doorway to greet her.

I wanted to do something for her, so I prayed for her speedy journey to The Light. I also called the horses to give her a swift ride to the Other Side. At some point, a sense of peace came over me. Wanting to do more for her, I gave her the gift of song. I sang patriotic songs like *America, the Beautiful* and holiday songs like *Silent Night* and *Joy to the World*. Some country songs came to my mind, and I sang them as well. I hummed a lullaby for a while. I sang every song I could think of (including some old Irish folk songs). The last song I sang to her was *Country Roads* by John Denver.

I thought she'd like it because it talked about going home and simple life stuff, like where she grew up. After several hours, I was tired, and the songs stopped coming to me. I went home to rest.

My phone rang early the next morning, before sunrise. It was the hospice nurse letting me know my mom appeared to be taking her last breaths. I woke my brother, and we rushed out the door. I was saying . . . "Hang on Momma, I'm coming!" because I wanted to tell her goodbye and didn't want her to die alone. Then the thought, "No, don't hold her here!" came to me. Right then I told her, "It's okay, mom. You go whenever you want. We'll be okay, and we love you."

My brother turned on the radio in his truck as we headed out to the nursing home. The current song playing was ending. The next song that came on was *Country Roads* by John Denver! I let my brother know I hadn't heard that song in ages and I had sung it to Mom the previous night (this "coincidence" didn't register in my brain at that moment).

Once we arrived at the nursing home, the staff told us our mother had passed away. They were getting her ready so we could see her. We were too late to say our last goodbyes and ensure she had loved ones by her side when she died. Since I had told her it was okay for her to go when she was ready, I didn't lay any guilt on myself over it. It comforted me to know we had really said our goodbyes the night before.

Although I wanted her to have loved ones with her, I think she did as she already had one foot on the Other Side when I was with her the previous evening.

I asked the nurse what time they pronounced her, and she told me. Later that day, I checked my phone to see what time the nurse had called. I wanted to know the approximate time I had heard the John Denver song. It was the same time my mom had died! The epiphany hit me and I felt like, duh! She was crossing over and sent me the song letting me know she was going Home, "Take me home . . . country roads". It was also letting me know she had heard everything I'd talked about and every song I'd sung to her the night before.

"It seems we don't get over a loss of major proportions."

My mom died at sunrise on a Friday morning the week before Thanksgiving. It was a beautiful sunrise! The sky was brilliant with red, orange, and blue hues cast upon the clouds. Multi-colored autumn leaves were lit up from the sun's rays. The leaves reminded me of the changing seasons, all things returning to Earth, and new beginnings. As I took in the beauty that celebrated her going Home, I remembered the time she visited me in Utah and asked me to sing an Irish song at her funeral. The song I sang was a folk song titled *The Green, White, and Gold.*

One of the songs I had sung for her the evening before she passed over.

The weather was cool and cloudy (with misting rain) the day of my mom's funeral. I said to my sister, "It's going to be sunny." She gave me a skeptical look, but I knew the Sun would come out and the rain would stop. I couldn't bring myself to wear black to the funeral, so I chose a light-colored dress suit. My eulogy was short, and I followed it up with the Irish song I had promised to sing for her years before. It was a wonderful service. Many people said nice things about her. Her favorite songs were played, and a montage of photographs viewed from her life. It felt like I was an observer instead of a participant.

The misty rain continued as the line of vehicles made their way to the memorial park to lay her to rest. All the mourners were waiting in silence until they placed her coffin in the mausoleum. Once placed, the graveside services would end. That's what we expected to happen, not what happened. The mausoleum space wasn't large enough to fit an urn and a casket! We waited on the manager to arrive and solve the dilemma. His solution was to open my mother's casket and place my brother's urn in it!

This was my breaking point. I had been strong and held myself together (mostly) until this turn of events. My knees went weak, and I began sobbing. Not sure why the reopening of her casket made me lose it. I guess my mental health, self-preservation mode was thinking, "Just one more step, and it's done."

When that didn't happen, the relief valve for my dangerous levels of stress turned on. I wondered why we
couldn't even have a funeral without some type of drama.

My nephews stood in front of her casket so the onlookers wouldn't see what was taking place. (No one wants to
see a previously laid to rest body.) My youngest brother
placed his older brother's urn inside the casket with our
mother. The casket was closed, and the mausoleum
workers again used their lift to reach the last resting place
for my mom and brother.

As my mom's coffin was being lifted and placed inside
the mausoleum, the gray clouds parted and the sun came
out! I looked at my sister and said, "Told ya!". My sister
came back with something like "It's a message from
Mom". I said, "Yep." Now that I've had time to reflect, I
think the Sun broke through the clouds because my mom
was finally happy. She was with her daughter, her parents, and her son. Once my mom's coffin was safely inside the mausoleum, the sun once again disappeared behind gray clouds.

The world I knew became strange after Mom passed.
There were no more holiday dinners at her house. Mother's Day, Birthday, Thanksgiving, and Christmas celebra-
tions were a thing of the past. The traditions we had held
for so long just ceased to exist. One day, I sat down with
my brother and we talked about what we should do about
this huge void in our lives. We decided we'd make our
own traditions with the life we had now.

We couldn't sit around and be miserable because things weren't the same anymore.

Along with my sister and nephew, I visited mom on the first anniversary of her death. The day was cool and cloudy, with drizzling rain. We placed three white roses in her vase. (The white rose is a symbol of mourning for me. I first used it at my grandma's funeral thirty-four years prior. They seemed appropriate for my mom as well.) After we placed the vase into its holder, the clouds parted and the sun came out! Was it simply a coincidence? We didn't think so. We believed it was a sign from our mother letting us know she appreciated the visit.

It seems we don't get over a loss of major proportions. I think we get through it and reshape our lives around what is now. Maybe we become stronger because the loss taught us some stuff about them and ourselves. We definitely find out we can be strong and resilient. We are often more strong and more brave than we ever imagined.

I have not been back to the mausoleum where my brother and mother lay side-by-side. I believe their spirits went Home and they aren't there. My mom and brother wouldn't want me to continue going there and reliving the misery year after year. They would want to see me happy and living my life. They were an integral part of the things I learned and experienced that led me to my life's work.

Now, you may not believe in a song sent to a loved one by a deceased relative.

You may not believe in archangels, the ability of a person's spirit to affect the weather, or any of the supernatural stuff I've shared in this chapter, but I lived it. It all happened, just like the time I felt the exact moment my nephew rode the horses Home.

What My Mom Taught Me

1. Being a racist isn't right.
2. Don't be two-faced.
3. There's nothing wrong with being "country".
4. Don't be a hypocrite.
5. If you carry hatred, guilt, remorse, worry, or greed in your heart, it will manifest as disease.
6. One of the hardest things in life is when a parent buries their child.
7. Older people know stuff. They've been there, done that. Take the time to listen to them. Don't think you know it all, because you don't.
8. Being raised on a farm doesn't prepare you for living in the city.
9. Society and laws were a lot different in my mom's day and there was a huge double standard for women.
10. Men didn't get in trouble for beating their wives back then.
11. Sometimes you never get over a trauma suffered young, and it affects the rest of your life IF you allow it to.
12. Love your children equally well.

13. We all have regrets. Try your best to set things right before you leave this world.

We follow our heart . . . once we learn how.

Once we understand the difference between what is expected and what we want to do.

Some learn this early in life . . . others later . . . some never.

I follow my heart, and it is red.
I do it because it is me, and I am it.

It's the part that makes me whole.
The part that removes the loneliness man knows.

When I walk the Red Road, I'm never alone.
I know All Things are a part of me.

There is never JUST me.

I follow my heart, and it is red.
Where else would I go?

13
Spiritual Awakening

So far, my life has been unique. I believe we all have unique stories about growing up, what we've experienced, and where we are today. Below, I summarize the experiences that prepared me to become what I am. It's the *Cliff Notes* version of the knowledge, skills, and experience I've gained in life. My intent is to show the pattern of events that helped me understand why I am here. It's also to assist you in seeing the patterns in your life that explain why you are here.

"Over the years, I took many a fine church for a test drive."

As a child, I remember knowing things far beyond my years. I can't tell you how I knew. I would get a gut feeling, hear or see something. My attention would focus on things others didn't notice. I had a tendency to listen more than I talked.

Perhaps this was (in part) because my home and school life required keen observation skills and silence.

I tried to fit into what family, society, school, and peers expected. I was forever feeling like an outsider or oddball. Have you ever felt alone in a room full of people? That's how I felt growing up. This feeling of aloneness stemmed from not being like other kids. I also got plenty of practice being a ghost at home. My mind was active, pondering possibilities on various topics and always coming up with questions. I was looking for answers and building my knowledge base. Besides improving my street smarts and doing well in school, I dove into religious studies.

Over the years, I took many a fine church for a test drive (Catholic, Pentecostal, Baptist, Full Gospel, Protestant, Church of Christ, and Lutheran). I would read a Bible passage and need clarification, so I would ask the Sunday School teacher, deacon, or pastor. They would give me an answer which made me ask more questions. Sometimes I'd quote a verse and ask why it seemed to contradict another verse or sermon.

Well, sometimes all my questions caused a bit of discomfort in said church leaders. I think maybe they thought I was stirring up trouble when I'd say, "That's not what the Bible says." It could be they believed they should see children, not hear them. I do not know. Anyway, all my questioning wore out my welcome at many churches. They didn't seem to understand that I was just curious. My logical mind was trying to make sense of it all.

My intuition would tell me if the answer wasn't quite right or if they made something up just to appease me. I also knew when I had gone over my daily quota of questions and it was time to be "quiet as a church mouse".

Some people have assumed I'm not familiar with the Bible. I don't talk about it much, but I've read the Bible from cover to cover. My baptism was conducted in a Southern Baptist church, where I also sang in the choir. Whether it was a revival, Vacation Bible School, Wednesday night supper, Sunday School, Sunday Service, or a fundraiser, I would be there. For many years, I studied and tried to make sense of the difference between Bible verses, sermons on a said verse, and the various church rules. After all my experiences with the various churches, I decided religion didn't sit well with me. My study of religion gradually turned into seeking spiritual answers.

". . . I didn't want the weird looks from people (or to watch their eyes glaze over)."

My spiritual studies didn't really begin until after I had my "crazy, white girl, mental breakdown". The day I sat outside crying during that thunderstorm was the turning point in my spiritual awakening. Like most people, my parents frowned upon my childhood spiritual connection. They forced me to hide it away it for many years.

As I've said before, I began reading Native American history and culture written by natives or translated by trusted authors. I learned a lot about the "Taming of the Wild West" and the "Indian Wars". Trying to find my place in the world, I started soaking up everything Indian.

Life works in mysterious ways, and I recognized my new life path from the first book I noted earlier: *Spirit Song* by Mary Summer Rain. I read their conversations and took in the lessons they shared. The words and advice resonated with me like nothing I'd experienced since feeling so natural playing the Indian as a child. The old saying, "You'll know it when you see it" rang true. My intuition was absolutely screaming at me! I felt a sense of peace (and homecoming) fill me up. The words spoke to me about things that had been a part of me for as long as I could remember. That book was what I needed (at the time) to affirm my life's direction, and I've never looked back. I'll always be grateful that the book crossed my path, a path that took many years to travel.

Once I started learning all I could about Indian culture, I morphed into having a workday persona and an at-home persona. A Lakotah word that best describes (to me) this dual persona is "anogete" (roughly translated means a woman with two faces). This word seemed to describe me perfectly. On the one hand, I was quiet and contemplative, the other a public speaker.

I would do what they expected of me at my day job, then come home and learn/experience the spiritual side of life. My beliefs, practices, diet, and everything else slowly changed into a walking contradiction of the frame of reference most people have of an American Indian.

Although I'd believed all my life I had native blood, I didn't pretend to be an Indian. I simply adopted certain beliefs and practices because they felt right for me. There were only a few people I could talk to about spiritual or Indian topics, so I kept them to myself. Now and then, I'd share a little when I met someone. My struggle between sharing and being afraid of sharing was real. I wanted to share all I'd learned with the entire world, but I didn't want the weird looks from people (or to watch their eyes glaze over). Sometimes, just for fun, I imagined them running away screaming, thinking I was crazy or the devil incarnate. Yep, I was indeed a closet Indian!

Eventually, my studies led me to want to discover my purpose and direction in life. I decided I needed to do a Vision Quest. The odds stacked against me, but everything fell into place. I completed two quests in Utah. My time spent high in the mountains praying, meditating, and dreaming will always remain special in my heart. At the end of my quests, I pledged to walk the Red Road (live a good life, help others, protect the Earth, honor the Ancestors, and honor all of creation). It was a decision I've done my best to honor to this day.

Eventually, I left Utah to live in Oregon. After four years in Portland, my family dynamics changed, and I moved back to my hometown. The same place fear had driven me from over twenty years prior. Although my home state was more enlightened or open than I remembered it being, it still had some growing to do. Nothing against Arkansas, but the predominant religion had a lot of folks believing spiritual stuff was the "devil's work" or "against the scriptures". My belief is people can believe anything they want. That's what free will and walking your own path are about.

A little over a year after I moved back home, I bought a house. Once I got settled into my new home, the childhood "knowing" started coming back. At first, random events happened that didn't seem to be caused by anything in particular. As time went on, the frequency of these events increased. Within three years, I was experiencing a lot of "paranormal" happenings, such as hearing, seeing, knowing, and smelling things others did not.

The first major event occurred on a sultry August afternoon. I was sitting on the porch reading a local publication called *AY Magazine*. It had a section called *Murder Mystery*, which I found interesting. That month's article was *Lives Lost & Found*. The article summarized unidentified person cases in Arkansas that were still unsolved. As I finished reading the first summary (feeling bad for the person and their family), I heard a name!

At first, I didn't understand why a name had popped into my head. I brushed it off and continued to read the next summary. As I finished the second case summary, I heard another name! I was freaking out a little, but I wrote the two names I'd heard next to their respective summary. By the time I finished the article, I had heard three or four names.

"How did I ever make it out of that shit storm?"

I remember my thoughts wandering and my mind coming up with questions as I read each summary. One question, "Who are these people?" was foremost on my mind as I read the article. I hadn't asked God or Jesus to reveal their names. Their names simply came to me, like the people who'd died agreed to pass them on to me. Yeah, you bet I was a little freaked out! My mind must have been open and calm so I could receive the messages. (Or maybe by thinking the questions, I was asking God to answer them.) There's no doubt I heard the names. It was as if someone had been there beside me, talking to me as I read!

In my state of shock (or disbelief), I didn't know what to do with the information I'd received. I let it simmer for a few days, but what to do still eluded me.

If I had shared this with someone (at the time), it may have helped me figure out what to do, but I was afraid of ridicule if someone asked me HOW I came across the information. Finally, I tore the article from the magazine and put it on my bookshelf. Time passed, and the article got buried beneath other papers, but I never threw it away. Each time I cleaned off the bookshelf, I would keep the article.

Time passed, spiritual experiences kept happening, and I filed away the article for later. The next April, my friend invited me to the Body, Mind & Soul Expo at the Peabody Hotel in Little Rock. Some might call it a "Psychic Fair" or a new age type show. At the expo, I had an aura photograph taken, which explained what my photo colors meant. Basically, the explanation stated that I had a lot of psychic/spiritual gifts and abilities. My mind went racing back to the *AY Magazine* article still in my filing cabinet.

I met a few practitioners at that event and started taking classes and exploring everything spiritual. I guess I wanted to understand all the experiences I'd been having, what my gifts were, and how to use them. My paranormal experiences became more frequent. I was seeking understanding and healing on many levels, and with that came "strange".

The strange things I experienced over the next seven years could fill a book! After a while, those experiences transformed from strange to normal.

The random events became an everyday part of life. My confidence grew, and I was no longer afraid to answer questions about how I got my information. I passed along the names I "heard" from reading that *AY Magazine* article! I hope it helped bring closure or answers to those families.

In those years, I also learned a lot about myself, my past, and my spiritual side. I grieved over the loss of two of my family members. Eventually, I became a vendor at the expo I had attended a year or two before! The more I used my spiritual gifts, the stronger they became. I also taught classes for others who wanted to learn about living a more spiritual life.

Sometimes my learning, practicing and teaching seemed like a long and winding road. I was a lonely traveler, not knowing where the road would lead. The constant feeling of aloneness stayed with me until I realized I wasn't simply dropped off to fend for myself. My logical conclusion was if I were here all alone, I wouldn't have survived my childhood, an abusive husband, and all the other trauma in my life. I certainly wasn't strong enough to prevent my child abuse. I had no control over being a passenger in an aircraft where smoldering electrical wires put us in grave danger of fire (or explosion) and nosediving to the ground at incredible speeds. Was it luck or destiny?

Have you ever been involved in an accident (or incident), and after the dust settled, you asked, "How did I ever make it out of that shit storm?". Okay, maybe you didn't put it exactly like that, but you know what I mean. Perhaps an ordinary day spun out of control so fast you watched it unfold in slow motion. Maybe a dangerous situation was going on all around you, but you came out of it without a scratch. Those types of events convinced me I had help and wasn't really alone at all!

The road I was on also helped me understand why I made it through all the stuff I experienced. Everything I'd learned and experienced in life made me uniquely qualified to live my purpose and passion! I needed to experience it all to get me to the place where I could help others with similar experiences. No one else has the unique perspective, skill set, or work experience as me (which is true for everyone).

My unique qualities led me to become a Spiritual Coach because I understood abuse, trauma, racism, addiction, poverty, religion, self-harm, and more. I worked through the past hurt, grief, pain, unworthiness, and confusion that negatively affected my life for so long. I learned how to become more than I believed I was for many years. In my heart, I wanted to assist others in doing the same. As a Spiritual Coach, I am doing just that . . . following my heart!

What I've Learned From My Life

1. Everything you've learned and experienced makes you uniquely qualified to do what you came here to do. So, do it!
2. No one else can do exactly what you can do for yourself and the world!
3. The past cannot haunt your present or future unless you allow it.
4. What happened to you as a child was beyond your control. What happens to you as an adult is all within your control.
5. Choose to release the hurt, pain, and grief.
6. We are all born with spiritual abilities or gifts. We choose whether we want to believe in or use them.
7. We are not alone! We have help. All we have to do is ask!
8. There are billions of possibilities for the path we choose to walk (one for each person). Don't be afraid to walk yours!
9. A simple way to be happy is to practice unconditional love, nourish your spiritual side, take care of the Earth, and nurture your unique gifts so they blossom into their full demonstration.
10. Never, ever give your power or Free Will away to others.
11. When you set your intent and are ready, doors will open for you!

12. You are loved. You are worthy! Don't allow others to tell you anything different.
13. Everything you think, say, do, and feel everyday comes back to you! Make them all positive!
14. Change the beliefs that no longer serve your Highest Good.

Lord, please guide my path.
Help me see through knowledgeable eyes.
Listen from compassionate ears.
Speak with wisdom.
Have a tender heart.

Conclusion

I could sit here and dwell upon how bad I had it growing up and all the struggles, but I'm really not sharing my story to host a pity party. Please don't feel sorry for me because of what I've experienced in life. I've shared my life's stories to share some insights into things I've learned, and hopefully one or two of them will help you.

When we're young, we may not know how bad we have it or that someone else always has it worse. When we're teenagers, we're convinced everything is dreadful and the entire world will end if we don't get those pants, shoes, or dress we want so badly. Everything is about you, and you don't see that other people struggle.

Having lived through several types of abuse, I see those happenings as helping shape me for my life's work. Without them, I wouldn't relate well to others, understand their point of view, or understand we all want the same stuff in life. I wouldn't be able to tell an abused person it wasn't their fault (and KNOW it wasn't).

There was nothing they could have done or said to make it better or go away. When we realize it's not our fault, and forgive ourselves for thinking it was, true healing can begin. We are often our own worst critics and punishers.

Some people will punish themselves for things they couldn't control. The reason they do this is that somewhere along the way, they started believing they were lacking. They started believing they were not good enough, smart enough, handsome, or pretty enough. So they became someone they're not to make up for these false beliefs. When they look in the mirror, they don't recognize the person staring back. Worse yet, they avoid looking into the mirror at all.

I sometimes envision funny happenings, and the angels and God are not exempt or taboo from these musings. (Remember, I am a closet comedian at heart.) In my world, the celestial beings enjoy a good laugh just like we do. For instance, one time I asked God to help me find an Inipi (Purification Ceremony). Four days later, a friend invites me to an Inipi that weekend! I accept the invitation. Later I'm telling friends about what happened and a funny movie plays in my head.

In this movie, I had declined the invitation to the Inipi and God was reacting to my decision. He appeared to me, and seemed irritated about something. He asked me, "Do you remember asking me to help you find an Inipi?" I said, "Yes". (He's waiting for me to get it.)

"Your friend invited you to a ceremony this weekend, and you said no". I nod my head in agreement. (This time a tinge of disappointment crosses his face, as he lets me know I'm still not getting it.) Then God said, "You asked me to help you find an Inipi. I line up the whole deal in four days, and you just say no"? He observes my lightbulb moment as I finally realize what I have done. I experience one of those big "oops!" moments. He just shakes his head.

My friends thought this make-believe story was hilarious because we'd all had our "duh!" moments. One of the most important abilities we can nurture is a sense of humor. We won't always connect the dots at the right time. Things won't always go our way. We may make poor decisions. Good thing God and the angels have lots of patience. If I were my Guardian Angel, I'd probably ask to be reassigned.

Anyway, the Creator knows his children better than they know themselves. He knows they are going to get into trouble and make questionable decisions. He may want a break sometimes, so he has all his other angels help him watch over us. God doesn't want us to die before we complete our life's mission. For some, they may complete their mission in a short time. For others, it may take them a very long time. Maybe our Guardian Angels and guides are glad they don't have to watch over us as long as they did Moses!

I tell this story to let you know you're not alone. You have help, so if you need it, ask! You are safe and protected! And the best part is you are loved! So, don't allow anyone to convince you of being not good enough. We were all created perfect, it's how we came into this world. Simply practice remembering how you came into this world (full of excitement, exploring, having fun, loving, and just BEING YOU). It's not gone forever unless you allow it.

Life can be rough, but don't allow it to stay that way. You can choose any moment to change and remember your authentic self. How we deal with our lives comes in many forms. We all have an escape . . . something that makes us feel better. For me, it has always been music and dancing. When I was afraid or hurt, I'd listen to a song to pick me up. The times when I dared not make a sound, I'd play a song in my head. It seems I sang from the time I was a little girl. Music was my calming, happy, go-to place. Having something that lifts your spirit is a good thing.

You've probably heard the Lord works in mysterious ways. Well, a few years ago, I discovered the name of my Guardian Angel. Immediately, my lifelong love of music made perfect sense. I hadn't realized what was in front of me my entire life. My Guardian Angel turned out to be the Angel of Music! I kid you not! Just then, I realized why I loved *The Phantom of the Opera*. (Hope you caught that one.)

Now who, but God, would know the exact angel I needed to help me through my rough times? This is just one example of how the Lord works in mysterious ways.

You may live your life according to what you know and believe (working a nine-to-five job with kids, a spouse, pets, and a minivan). There is absolutely nothing wrong with that way of living. But one day, you may wake up and feel something is missing. You won't be able to shake it. You can try to keep your mind busy, but the feeling will return in quiet moments. If you're not living your passion and purpose . . . it will come.

Don't be afraid. It's just an auto-reminder you've set for yourself. It's reminding you to finish your mission or purpose. Some people believe their purpose is this huge undertaking. Everyone's purpose is different. One person may have a mission that includes several small things. Another person may have a purpose with one big thing. See?

Don't think you have to do your purpose a certain way, either. You should go about completing your mission YOUR way. There are many roads you can take to your destination. How you get there is up to you. Trust your instincts. Learn, grow, and have fun with it! You were born with the inherent knowledge built-in. Remember, you lack nothing! You simply need to remember to TRUST . . . LOVE . . . BE . . .

Am I the perfect person now with no worries or drama? No, I continue to work on my past when it comes up.

Every day I practice patience, understanding of myself and others, and my spiritual beliefs. I CAN tell you that my life differs completely from what it was before. There is more happiness, creativity, prosperity, and less drama than ever before.

On my first Vision Quest, I made a promise I have done my best to keep. Although I've kept a regular job to pay bills, I never went back to the keeping up with the Jones' lifestyle. I didn't buy into having all those initials after my name. I haven't looked back despite some rough spots along the way. If I could give everyone one piece of advice, it would be to stop looking back! Release any old stuff you've been carrying around that no longer serves your Highest Good. Look ahead and do the things that bring you joy!

Life Stuff I've Learned

1. Anyone who abuses you (in any way) won't stop, so it won't get any better. You cannot change them. THEY have to change themselves. If you stay, it will be a continuous cycle of apology, good behavior, tension, escalation, and then more abuse. Sometimes they will kill. You deserve better than this!

2. You cannot fix a person with a drug or alcohol addiction. They will remain addicted until THEY decide to tackle the root cause of their addictive behavior. You cannot change them or save them.

You can only change or save yourself. They will take you down with them. You deserve better than this!

3. You cannot change or stop a person's criminal behavior. A person will continue behaviors until THEY decide to change themselves. They will take you down with them. You deserve better than this!

4. Don't focus on things you have no control over. It's a fool's errand. Focus on what you have control over . . . you!

5. Fix you and love you! Only by knowing and loving yourself will you have the energy and love to give to others who deserve it.

6. Everyone deserves to be loved, happy, safe, warm, fed, housed, and have a career. Yes, this means you too! Regardless of what you may have been told, don't settle for anything less. Don't believe you deserve anything less.

7. Have fun, do new stuff, learn new stuff, and experience life!

8. Send love to everyone and everything in creation. Love is stronger than any negative emotion. Let go of fear and put love in its place.

Please Leave a Review!

If you enjoyed *Born a Poor, Black, Indian, White Girl*, please leave a review at your favorite bookstore with this link:
books2read.com/u/bWQMGW

It would mean a lot to me and I read every review!

How Can Spiritual Change Your Life?

Check out De's *Simple Spiritual Journey* books! Just go to her website at DeFletcher.com and sign up to be notified when her next book hits the bookstores!

Also by De Fletcher

The Truth About Spiritual Gifts reveals truths about our inherent knowledge, how we were mislead about our spiritual nature, and how to use our hidden gifts to create the life we know we deserve!

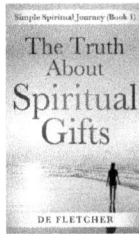

Pick up a copy of The Truth About Spiritual Gifts today!
https://books2read.com/u/b5o1ok

Not ready to buy? Check out an excerpt from the book here:
https://www.bktry.com/G2CR1wZx

OR

Sign up for new releases and perks and get 2 chapters free!
https://Spirit-Truths.gr8.com

About the Author

De is best known for her unique ability to blend humor, realism, and simplicity into her books, coaching, and public speaking.

She grew up poor, living in racially divided cities and on a rural farm. As a child, De experienced racism, bullying, abuse, addiction, and death. As an adult she experienced the culture, language, and traditions of 15 countries and 25 US states. Those experiences reflect in her writing, humor and interaction with others.

Embracing her wildly diverse life experiences enables her to relate to her reader's and truly "get" where they are coming from.

The real-life stories, spiritual knowledge, and experience she shares are a result of her twenty-plus-year professional and spiritual journey.

De is an independent author and professional trainer with 20 years of writing, public speaking, teaching, and coaching experience. She holds a Master of Education Degree from Weber State University.

De is currently an author, speaker, and coach of living a simple, spirit-full life.
Learn more about De at DeFletcher.com

Go to https://defletcher.com/sign-up/ to sign-up for tips, exclusives, insider firsts, polls, cover reveals, and perks for upcoming books!

Connect with De at:
https://www.linkedin.com/in/defletcherauthor/

Watch De's Vids!
Go to spirituallife.locals.com and join my spiritual learning community!
Watch free content or subscribe and get 30 days for free!
Use code: **30FREE**

Follow De at your favorite bookstore!
books2read.com/DeFletcher Click the "Follow this Author" button to see my *Reading List* and get notified when I publish my next book!

https://www.amazon.com/author/defletcher

https://www.bookbub.com/authors/de-fletcher

Acknowledgments

A big thanks to Dave Chesson at Kindlepreneur, David Gaughran, JoAnna Penn of The Creative Penn, Mark Dawson of Self Publishing Formula, and Jeffrey Bruner at The Fussy Librarian for all the tips and tools they graciously give to authors that helped me create a better book for my readers.

I want to acknowledge my launch team (Linda, Vandra, Theresa, Lisa, Catherine, Joshua, and Jennifer). Thank you for sharing your time, skills, vision, and encouragement! You helped me get my book out into the world and into as many people's hands as possible. You guys are great!

A special thanks to Matt Davies for a beautiful cover that fit the content of my book perfectly. You are an outstanding talent!

Finally, I am reaching out to Anna, my colleague at the Utah Department of Workforce Services . . . I still remember how you looked at me like I'd just had some crazy, white girl mental breakdown when I told you the name of my book all those years ago. It's finally here and I hope you enjoy it, chica! A toast to you, "Mi amiga loca de Puerto Rico!"

www.ingramcontent.com/pod-product-compliance
Lightning Source LLC
Chambersburg PA
CBHW060947050426
42337CB00052B/1628